Supernatural
and
Mysterious
Japan

Supernatural
and
Mysterious
Japan

Spirits, Hauntings,
and
Paranormal Phenomena

Catrien Ross

All photographs, unless otherwise noted, were taken
by the author.

YENBOOKS
2-6 Suido 1-chome, Bunkyo-ku, Tokyo 112

ISBN 4-900737-37-2
LCC Card No. 95-60909

First edition, 1996

Printed in Japan

Contents

Contents

Preface

There is always a beginning, and looking back, perhaps the idea behind this book first took hold in February 1993. At that time I was living in a run-down, traditional, Japanese-style house I had heard was connected with Koizumi Yakumo, also known as Lafcadio Hearn (1850–1904). Details of this link were hazy, but as a writer I liked to think of this drafty old structure as somehow having inspired that long-dead chronicler of Japan's ghostly and weird. Already I felt sad that I could only be here for a short time, and hoped I would find another place in the neighborhood.

Although the interior was inconvenient and cold, especially in winter, I had taken this room because the rent was reasonable for central Tokyo, and, what's more, my windows opened out to a large garden filled with birds and sheltering trees. Owned by the adjacent Buddhist temple, the house itself seemed to sit right in the cemetery, and coming home late at night, I was often startled by the wooden markers at graves clattering in the wind like old bones.

One morning I had just pulled shut the wooden gate and turned into the street, when I saw a Japanese woman who looked at me intently. We walked silently in the same direction for a few minutes, when suddenly she turned to me and asked, in English, "You are living in that old house?" I nodded, and she then explained that the house had been lived in by the Koizumi Yakumo family, and that she personally knew Lafcadio Hearn's grandson, and his beautiful wife. She also knew their son, who was now in Matsue, Shimane Prefecture, researching his famous great-grandfather. The woman, Shizuko, was also from Matsue, but her father had bought land here in Tokyo some thirty-five years ago. She seemed delighted to learn I was from Scotland, because twenty years previously she had lived with her husband in London, and among her most precious memories was a journey to Scotland, and a visit to the Edinburgh Festival.

At the station she introduced me to a waiting friend, and the three of us boarded the train together. Just before Shizuko got off, she asked me how long I would be staying in the house. I said I would soon be leaving, and while I had arranged the following month's accommodation, after that I did not know where I would stay. Right there and then she offered me a house belonging to her father but now used by her niece, who was leaving to live in America for ten months. If I wanted the house, about an eight-minute walk away from my current home, she would check with her father, and we could talk again that evening.

Mulling over our extraordinary encounter, I called her back in the late afternoon, just to make sure it had all been real. She felt exactly the same way, and told me that for some reason she had felt overwhelmingly compelled to talk with me that morning, although I was a complete stranger and a foreigner, as well. Thinking things over, she concluded that the ghost of Lafcadio Hearn had arranged our meeting.

And so I moved into a house in the same neighborhood, a single-story, furnished dwelling with its own garden. On my first day there, a bird, just like one I had been feeding from my window, perched on my laundry pole and squawked loudly at me.

As I had experienced a number of strange happenings in what I named the "Koizumi house," the entire incident with Shizuko simply fueled my growing awareness of the hidden currents that move beneath the surface of everyday life. In fact, 1993 turned out to be not only a year of the increasingly mysterious, but also a major, personal turning point. By the end of the year my life had changed dramatically, and my involvement with the supernatural and Japan's world of "superpower," as supernatural abilities are often called in Japan, became intense and irrevocable.

One evening I returned to the Koizumi house to find a Japanese man, Abe Yukio, waiting for me at the cemetery. Several months before, he had by chance picked up the telephone when I was calling about renting the house, and we had briefly talked, but not yet met in person. Now he had come to talk with me about Oriental medicine, which I was researching for an article. Although we did not have contact again until many months later, when he came to treat my backache, today he and I run a clinic together in Nishi Hachioji. I am a healer who also gives therapy involving the analysis and adjustment of the patient's flow of *ki,* the natural energy that fills the entire universe. A former Soto Zen monk, Abe is a specialist in traditional Oriental medicine, licensed in Japanese adjustment, acupuncture, and chiropractic. Another eventful encounter. Another transforming shift.

When I first came to Japan in October 1987, the last thing I expected to research was the supernatural. Like so many foreigners, I had come initially for business reasons. I was an official member of a U.S. State of Arizona economic mission that had come to Asia to open a trade office in Taipei, Taiwan, and had stopped over in Japan almost as an afterthought. From the moment I arrived here, I felt Japan was special for me, a reaction common to many foreigners, who tend to instantly like or dislike this apparently westernized Asian nation. I liked Japan enough to know that I wanted to live here, if only to try to unlock the secret of this strong attraction.

Once I finally started my research into Japan's supernatural leanings, including a personal exploration of the dimension of *ki*, I found many new doors opening, and all manner of connections being easily and widely made. Being of mystical bent, I am inclined to think that this was as it should be, and that I had stumbled onto what was, for me, the right path.

My first efforts began, unlikely as it may seem, at the Ministry of International Trade and Industry (MITI). There, an old friend, Matsufuji Tetsuo, then at the ministry-affiliated Agency of Industrial Science and Technology, helped me set up meetings with ministry officials concerning supernatural research conducted by MITI. If I was surprised to discover MITI's hardheaded bureaucrats investigating the otherworldly, I soon found that at the personal level, the spiritual quest is quite sincere. Thanks to Tsunoda Yoshisue, then at Japan's New Sunshine Program to develop alternative energy sources and uses, I was invited to join MITI's weekly *ki ko* class. This in turn led to my getting to know the instructor, Nakamura Akira, a lay monk and founder of Toyo Bunka Study Group, who two years later has graced this book with his fine sumi-e illustrations.

It was at the Agency of Industrial Science and Technology that I was invited to a meeting with Uri Geller, who demonstrated his telepathic talents and of course bent a teaspoon, which I still have. I was to meet him again twice that year, and learned that Japanese companies have been using his perceived powers in seeking new business opportunities. In the fall of 1993 I met the decidedly eccentric Masaki Kazumi, who did not look at me when I entered the room, instead averting his gaze as he motioned for me to sit down. He then took his pendulum and a sheet of paper and immediately began analyzing my *fuchi* pattern, as he calls his divination method. Told many things about myself, I also learned the age at which I would die. Masaki released this potentially upsetting information because he said I had a chance to increase my life span by twenty-five years, provided I make some changes. Before I left his cramped laboratory, where a machine is continuously set up to catch signals from outer space, he presented me with a four-leaf clover, two books, and his "Para Memory" machine. Touted as a brain-wave-enhancer and entryway to past lives, it gave me an instant headache, and has been gathering dust ever since, its promise of insight into past lives unfulfilled.

Accompanying Nishino Kozo to his classes at his school in Shibuya, I watched displays of his *ki* power, which really do have to be seen to be believed. A man of tangibly vital force, despite the fact that he used to smoke 150 cigarettes a day, Nishino appeared at his interview wearing a peach suit with gold buttons, a pink belt, a white sports shirt, and Japanese wooden sandals. Well-known and respected in the world of ballet, he has established a school of breathing techniques that is extremely organized and obviously successful, although I had the feeling that his students and instructors, while developing their awareness, are definitely followers rather than future pioneers in the world of *ki*. But perhaps there is only room for one Nishino.

By contrast, Kurita Masahiro comes across as much quieter, although equally dedicated to helping people realize their *ki* potential. At one of his regular lectures in Ikebukuro, I watched Kurita use his hands to heal aches and pains among the attendees. He believes his creation of the "Super Reading System," which greatly enhances speed reading skills, is a practical way to introduce people to the more esoteric philosophy of *ki* improvement. And I frequently see people doing Kurita's finger rotation exercises on the train or subway. Abandoning the life of a Buddhist monk for the study of mathematics and then medicine, Kurita has been involved in a lifelong mystic search. On the very last day of what had been a multiyear mystical training program, he was hit by a car on a mountain road as he was returning home. During the following months spent in hospital, he clearly formulated his way to teach people about *ki*.

Nomura Harehiko, meanwhile, has become a valued friend who regularly shows up at my home with his latest research results. In recent years, some scientists in the West have scathingly referred to proponents of the new physics as "Neo-Buddhists," as one discovery after another in the realm of physics brings the world of natural science ever closer to the universe of Eastern mysticism. Nomura, who happens to be a practicing Buddhist, as well as a physicist specializing in superconductivity, manages to balance fifteen-day mystical training fasts with rigorous scientific experiments. Through his efforts, and those of his open-minded associates, new and intriguing insights concerning the phenomenal and intimated worlds are continuously being observed. Such work creates a bridge between the known and the unknown.

Despite my helpful connections, I found that researching the mysterious and strange in Japan is not always an easy task. Outside of the world of mystics, for whom the mysterious is a part of daily life, most Japanese people are reluctant to discuss the supernatural, either out of superstitious caution, a desire for secrecy, or simple lack of interest. August may be the month to remember the dead and listen to eerie tales, but ghost stories that touch one personally can seem too close for comfort.

There is a dearth of information in English concerning Japan and the supernatural, so much of my research involved working with material that first had to be translated from the original Japanese. Since I do not yet read Japanese, most of this necessary translation work was generously undertaken by Abe Yukio. It was a was a time-consuming task, and, of course, the possibility for factual errors exists. Anyone who has worked closely with the Japanese language is aware of the frustrations inherent in translation. There is so much vagueness and ambiguity that trying to extract all the facts is very difficult, especially given the subject matter. Details of ghostly hauntings of places seem to be left deliberately vague, leaving much to the reader's imagination. While this may be the mark of a thrilling ghost story, it is not helpful for someone who wants to tell the tale in another language.

In addition, many regions in Japan have their own versions of the same story, so it was left up to me to select which details to include. Often, in the end, I decided that it was less important to know exactly when something happened than to accept that the story had become part of Japanese cultural lore, and therefore has its own significance. At the same time, it was a pleasure to learn just how much Japanese, like Scots, have always loved ghost stories. As a people, Scots are comfortable with the mystical, and psychic gifts are accepted, particularly among the communities of the northern Highlands and Islands. In Japan I did not have to stretch my imagination very far.

So many of us in the modern world are cut off from even simple, natural experiences like walking in a forest, or sitting by a mountain river. In the glass and steel edifices which protect us from the elements, we have forgotten the power of the wind, the strength of water. One of the reasons why I enjoy my present life in Japan is that I have been able to keep such experiences very near to me. I am now living in yet another old house, which has its own well and carp pond, and the vagaries of the weather, such as spectacular summer lightning storms, remind me that I walk in the shadow of Mount Takao.

This sacred mountain in Western Tokyo, with long-standing supernatural ties, has become a favorite place for *ki* exercising or mental refreshment. Early one morning, I was climbing the path as usual, when I heard drumming and strange chanting. In a small cave which serves as a shrine I saw three women. One was drumming and chanting, the second was leaning against the railing, and the third was kneeling inside the cave, rocking to and fro, and moaning. I watched as she emerged to dance around to the beat of the drum, like the Sun Goddess coming out of the cave in Japan's creation myth.

On the way back, I decided to walk down and introduce myself as a Scots shaman. The drummer grinned broadly and announced she was a Korean shaman, and that this was a special ritual to call down the gods for spirit possession. Another morning, with winter frost on the ground, I watched as a young man performed the austere purification ritual under the icy cascade of the Biwataki waterfall. Living in Japan constantly reinforces my perception that the mysterious and the magical shimmer at the edge of our ordinary existence. The extraordinary or the supernatural is within easy reach.

When I began looking into the supernatural, I had not planned to write a book, and the proposal from Tuttle was both timely and welcome. On the other hand, I found that writing a book is a major undertaking that requires the help of many people, all of whom I am unable to name. I give especial thanks to Abe Yukio for his patience and translations; to Hans Laetz for his generous search for materials in America; to Matsufuji Tetsuo for his historical insights and help with photographs and meetings; to Hayashibara Ken and Mohammad Raees for revealing meetings and wonderful talks; to Tsunoda Yoshisue and other MITI people for showing me the worlds of *ki ko* and aikido; and last, but not least, to Nakamura Akira—also known by his monk's name, Takuho—for his splendid imagination and sumi-e skills.

And now a word about my personal history. The oldest of five children, I am the product of the coming-together of two very different cultures. I was born in Jakarta, on the Indonesian island of Java, to an Indonesian mother and Scots father. When I was four years old we returned to live in Scotland, where tales of Scottish ghosts and Indonesian demons became part of our family lore; thinking about the supernatural was natural. This background, perhaps, has bequeathed to me an abiding curiosity and adaptability. In this next step of my life, I am in Nishi Hachioji running QRQ, a healing center, and creating a worldwide network of healers, alternative thinkers, and futurists. Somehow, for me, the supernatural, superpower, *ki,* the mystic search, strange coincidences, and unlikely happenings have all become part of the same, and for me essential, journey.

For the reader unfamiliar with Japan's supernatural, this book should provide a preliminary introduction to the shadowy world that lies behind Tokyo's hard, commercial dazzle. There may be readers who are disappointed that I did not include more, but to cover all was not my intent. As an exploratory journey into otherworldly things in Japan, this book is meant to offer a starting point. I hope readers will enjoy reading its pages as much as I have enjoyed writing them.

Supernatural and Mysterious Japan

CHAPTER ONE

In Search of the Supernatural

It is an eerie place. A barren moonscape of jagged rocks and no trees. Bubbling sulfur hot springs, some yellow, some blood-red, release the stink of rotten eggs into the gloomy air. Here and there, wisps of steam rise from cracks in stone that can be icy or hot to the touch. A short walk away, at the crater's center, a stretch of water known as Lake Usori gleams dark and still. Perhaps it is mere fancy, but standing on the shore, aptly called the "shore of paradise," the feeling is that if one were to set sail for the other side, there would be no return. In this murky water only one species of fish, a type of dace, can survive the acidic content. All around, the gray desolation, broken only by a few, hardy rhododendron bushes, could be a stage prop for an imagined scene from hell, or the most likely place for lost spirits to wander.

Such is the landscape of Mount Osore, a forbidding caldera (its name means "Dread") located near the tip of the axe-shaped Shimokita Peninsula in Aomori Prefecture, part of Japan's northern Tohoku region. Long considered sacred, it is supposedly a spot where the living and the dead can meet. In local idiom, those who have died have "gone to the mountain," and it is at this crater that contact can once again be made with family members who have long since left the human world. Today, this supernatural connection takes place during a special festival held twice a year. The main event is the summer Osorezan Jizo Festival, held in Mutsu City, from July 20–24, with a second festival held from October 9–11. At these times, Mount Osore is lit by some forty lanterns, which flicker ghostlike through the night.

People anxious to communicate with the spirits of dead relatives head here from all over Japan to consult with the area's shamanistic mediums, traditionally blind, old women known as *itako*. Usually a girl novice enters *itako* training before her first menstruation. She then spends several years learning chants, prayers, and a form of fortunetelling. Once she completes the ritual known as *kamitsuke*, in which she goes into a trance, she is believed to have entered a holy marriage, *shinkon*, and is thereafter qualified to become an independent practitioner. At the July festival especially, many *itako* gather at Mount Osore's main gate to perform for visitors as mediums in an activity called *kuchiyose*, or speaking in the voice of the dead.

Reasons why people come to this supernatural setting are numerous: a yearning for remembrance, comfort from grief, psychological problems, or simply a desire for advice or reassurance. When she is given specific information such as a name, the medium begins keening in a singsong voice to initiate the trance that can transport her to limbo, where she will search for the designated soul and possibly bring back a message. Sometimes her voice abruptly changes, or her pattern of moving shifts, indicating that spirit contact has been made and a message is coming through. Unfortunately, any communications from the spirit world are relayed in a northern dialect so thick that even natives of this area have difficulty understanding. Nevertheless, many people leave Mount Osore satisfied that they have indeed reached the spirits of, say, a dead spouses or children.

What mysteries might lie across the water from Mount Osore's "shore of paradise"? (Photo courtesy of Aomori Prefectural Government)

Not that all requests are successful, of course. Some visitors, for instance, lose courage at the last moment and instead of calling up souls of dead people whom they knew personally, escape by asking about some well-known Japanese politician instead. One man reportedly asked about Marilyn Monroe, to whom he had no relation at all. Given the mystery of the afterlife, perhaps people feel it's safer that way.

When the hectic festivals are over, the *itako* return to their village homes, where they continue to be quietly consulted throughout the year on tasks ranging from calling down household gods (families in this region have personal household gods), to healing the sick. If a person falls ill, an *itako,* as shaman, can attempt to identify the spirit that is causing the sickness. If she is successful, she rids the body of the intruder, thus curing the patient of the disease.

But shamanic traditions and ancient folk beliefs are not the only religions evident at this centuries-old holy spot. Mount Osore is also home to the Entsuji temple, established in 845, and now run by the Soto sect of Zen Buddhism. This major Zen discipline was founded in Japan by Dogen (1200–53) after his return from China in 1227. The temple buildings are dispersed among the sulfur springs and rock outcrops, and there are also wooden bathhouses, free for anyone to use.

Buddhist influence shows in the numerous Jizo (one of the Bodhisattva) statues encountered between the main temple buildings and Lake Usori. Jizo is the guardian deity of children, so when the summer visitor season ends, his statues are typically covered with offerings of infant-sized clothing, as well as food, drink, and small toys. These gifts are meant to aid him in taking care of children who have died and are struggling to reach the next world. One of his jobs is to make nightly rounds of the rocky riverbed which lies between this world and the next, a stretch of land known as the Sai no Kawara. As he walks around at night, he encourages the yet-homeless spirits, who are busily piling up small mounds of stones, to enter paradise. At the same time, he frightens away the malevolent demons who delight in constantly knocking down the stone piles the spirits have so painstakingly built. Visitors to Mount Osore often add a stone or two to existing piles, or construct new ones, as a way of lending a helping human hand to the unseen spirit world. Because Jizo's sandals soon wear out on the rocks of the riverbed, offerings of straw sandals are also commonly left at the feet of his statues.

From mystic Mount Osore, it is a 1,380-kilometer journey south, as the crow flies, to a supernatural display of a very different sort.

In the city of Nagasaki on Kyushu, Japan's third largest island, there is a small cafe called Andersen, situated on the second floor of the building next to the bus terminal at Kawadana Station. Andersen is run by Hisamura Toshihide, a fortyish man of earnest demeanor who claims supernatural ability in the form of psychokinetic power, *nengurafii* in Japanese. Hisamura's reputation is such that it now draws people from throughout the country, and there are almost always taxis waiting to whisk a stream of curious visitors to and from Nagasaki Airport, about a thirty-minute ride away. The cafe has become a venue for Hisamura's psychokinetic shows, staged three times daily, at 10 A.M., 2 P.M., and 6 P.M. With seven tables and one long counter, the cafe can seat only thirty customers, and once it is full, additional visitors must await the next show. Although there is no charge for the show itself, customers must order from a menu that offers standard Japanese-style coffee shop fare at regular prices, including curried rice with beef, and sandwiches. One requirement is that all customers must come with an open mind. Skeptics and naysayers are not welcome, and anyone who voices initial suspicion is asked to leave, a policy Hisamura justifies by noting that he does not charge for admission to the show.

After customers have eaten, the display begins. On a typical day, Hisamura, wearing an apron and rolling up his sleeves, joins his audience. A favorite opener is to ask for a customer's cigarette, which he places on his palm, where it levitates and jumps. When he places the same cigarette in a glass, it pops right out. Borrowing a watch, he stops the long hand at the time he specifies aloud. Again, using no hands, he sets another watch at a time requested by a customer. Someone in the audience is asked to touch Hisamura, who then slows or stops his own pulse. Another customer draws a picture, which Hisamura duplicates without ever seeing it. One government researcher who watched Hisamura's performance listed at least twenty-eight observed feats. A spoon bends or becomes a fork. Bolts bend. Coins grow bigger. Dice are controlled. Raw egg appears out of tissue paper. Paper money floats above Hisamura's hands or moves around inside a glass container.

Is all this really supernatural ability? Some critics dismiss Hisamura as a mere conjurer, and a shabby one at that. Others, among them the chairman of Sony Corporation, are impressed by his talents, convinced that his psychokinetic powers are genuine. A book about Hisamura's life details the history of his supernatural development and life philosophy, but the jury is still out. Meanwhile, Andersen customers continue to delight in his shows, enthusiastically oohing and aahing with each new feat. Viewing is limited, however. A notice on the wall requests anyone who has seen the show once to wait at least one month before returning. Someone who has seen him twice already is asked to come back at least three months later. Hisamura's reasoning is that other people should have a chance to see his free demonstrations of what he calls psychic mind over matter.

In examining the supernatural in Japanese society, it is important to bear in mind that the activities at Mount Osore and Andersen, while not exactly ordinary, are by no means rare. In fact, they are just two examples of the persistent fascination with the supernatural that has characterized Japanese culture from its beginning.

Elements of the supernatural permeate Japan's folklore and traditions, and a sense of the mysterious remains a dynamic force today. In a bustling megalopolis like Tokyo, where some twelve million people support the economic behemoth that is modern Japan, the search for the supernatural is easily obscured from the casual observer. A closer look, however, reveals that not only does interest in the supernatural endure, but in recent years it has actually increased as Japanese people have sought to combine their economic efforts with a striving for spiritual gratification. In the search for life's deeper meaning, a probe into the supernatural seems a natural progression.

Take the mass media, for example. The supernatural is one of the most popular topics in the entertainment world, and psychics and mediums make regular television appearances. Books on the paranormal become instant bestsellers, and entire magazines are now devoted to various psychic phenomena. Classes in the supernatural are sought after by everyone from college students to the elderly, and there is a burgeoning network of courses in psychic power enhancement. Some of these are linked to religious groups or associations, long known for their training in supernatural techniques. Others are headed by individuals who have undergone a personal, mystic experience. Indeed, self-appointed gurus of the supernatural abound, and sales of paraphernalia for developing individual psychic potential are brisk.

Each week, it seems, there is a growing number of advertisements for lectures in such subjects as psychokinesis, clairvoyance, telepathy, astral travel, channeling, and even UFO investigations. What's more, the roster of so-called ordinary people who have become psychic celebrities continues to swell. There is the *sarariiman* (white-collar, salaried employee) whose unexpectedly awakened healing gifts have brought him nationwide fame. A movie about his life has already been released. Another healer, a former veterinarian, cures a host of ailments using only his hands and eyes. Japanese television cameras follow a well-known medium as she trots the globe in her attempt to contact spirits of the dead.

In this nation where meditating monks exist side by side with staid-suited white-collar workers, esoteric mystic practices have never lost their appeal. Secretive sects and reclusive spiritual groups have existed for centuries, each with its own methods of tapping the supernatural. There is also an established history of bizarre cults, many of which are based on the perceived psychic power of their founders. Shake most religious sects and out will probably fall a leader with paranormal talents that initially attracted followers. In Japan the spiritual quest and supernatural awakening have often been synonymous.

In other words, the search for the supernatural is not a recent phenomenon. A look at the roots of Japanese mythology reveals that Japan brims over with gods and goddesses, resulting in what is known as the "rush hour of the gods." There are said to be eight million deities, who reside not only in Paradise, but also everywhere on earth. These deities, or *kami*, live in mountains, rivers, lakes, forests, rocks, and individual homes, according to the pantheon of Shinto, which literally means the "*kami* way." The term *kami* basically is a title for any honorable, sacred spirit, and since all beings have such spirits, anything can be a *kami*. They are thus believed to be represented by everything from Mount Fuji to the household cooking stove. They are even found in the toilet. In Japan the most lofty to the most mundane is endowed with supernatural properties.

Nor is every deity benevolent. Numerous demons, or *oni*, are thought of as malignant supernatural forces believed to mirror the dark side of human nature. Destructive to the world of humankind, these incarnate universal forces exert evil influence which must be guarded against or purified. Millions of Japanese people carry small charms to ward off demons or any misfortune they might cause. And a ritual of demon expulsion is carried out by many Japanese housewives as a way of marking the end of winter on a day called *setsubun*. Demons also represent natural forces such as wind and thunder, the storm spirits with their devastating anger.

To these native animistic beliefs, so closely linked with nature, have been added the deities of Buddhism, a religion which came to Japan around 552, bringing supernatural overtones from India, China, and Korea. A demon queller from China's Tang dynasty (618–907), for example, was readily adopted into Japanese folk mythology as Shoki. Later Buddhist portrayals of this entity depict him as one of hell's judges in the "hell scrolls," or *Jigoku-zoshi*, of Japan's Kamakura era (1185–1392). Another import from China were tales of the eight immortals of Taoism.

These were believed to be historical personages who had achieved human transcendence through rigorous refinement of body and mind into a supernatural state. As Zen Buddhist thought developed in Japan, these immortals came to symbolize intellectual and spiritual freedom.

Then there are the goblins. Japanese mountain temples often display the mask of the long-nosed goblin known as the *tengu.* The *tengu,* which looks like a ferocious Pinocchio, may have been introduced into Japan

This mask depicts a long-nosed *tengu,* or mountain goblin.

from India by way of China, and may derive from the Hindu Buddhist guardian Garuda, the mythical bird deity able to transform its shape. A messenger and helper to the gods, Garuda is also an enemy of serpents and demons. At the Todaiji temple in Nara, there are wooden masks of scowling bird heads and long-nosed men that are thought to have been carved in the seventh and eighth centuries. Now protected as "National Treasures," such masks were once used in *gigaku* performances, religious dances which originated in Tibet and India and arrived in Japan by way of Korea in 612. Although no longer danced today, *gigaku* were once considered the proper musical accompaniment to prayer in Japan's Buddhist temples.

With its magical powers, the *tengu* figures prominently in earlier Japanese folk tales and legends, and there are also close ties to Buddhist lore. In Japan, the *tengu* lost some of its fearsome and revered nature, becoming an impish goblin among whose favorite tricks was changing into the form of a Buddhist priest or nun, or even Buddha. In such guises, it would waylay unsuspecting monks, or lead them down the wrong path. Japanese *tengu* also evolved into two distinct types: *karasu tengu,* a crow-headed figure which has a body covered by feathers and long claws in the place of fingers and toes; and *konoha tengu,* the long-nosed kind. During the twelfth century, the concept of "*tengu* road" came to mean punishment in the form of exile for hypocritical or vainglorious Buddhist priests. Some say *tengu* are actually reincarnations of wicked priests who are being punished for being too proud or greedy.

Tengu are also associated with Japan's mountain priests or *yamabushi,* known even now for their magical, ascetic practices on holy mountains. In fact, *tengu* often wear the hexagonal hats of *yamabushi* and carry feather fans which they use for making themselves invisible or working other magic. Because these goblins dwell in mountains or high forests, rural villagers still make offerings to them before cutting down trees, or hold festivals in their honor. Trees themselves are thought to contain spirits that are usually benevolent, but sometimes inimical to human beings, so it is well to appease them, too, just in case.

Sometimes *tengu* are thought to cause illness, and they are said to have haunted Hojo Takatoki (1303–33), who committed suicide as the last Hojo regent of the Kamakura *bakufu*, or military government. Strongly criticized for preferring drinking to politics, in his later years he was constantly plagued by nightmares of aggressive *tengu*. Minamoto no Yoshitsune (1159–89), on the other hand, is said to have found *tengu* to be extremely helpful; legend has it that they taught him the secrets of martial arts and military strategy. Perhaps the greatest of all Japan's popular heroes, Yoshitsune is celebrated in the *Heike Monogatari (Tale of the Heike)*, created in the early thirteenth century. This epic war tale, which has much in common with the European *Song of Roland*, recounts the battle between the Heike and Minamoto clans, with Yoshitsune fighting for the victory of the Genji over the Taira. Recited to successive generations of listeners, the *Heike Monogatari* illustrates idealized warrior-class behavior against a backdrop of Buddhist attitudes and ethics.

At the age of seven, Minamoto no Yoshitsune was sent to study at the temple founded in 770 on Kyoto's Mount Kurama. There, in the Valley of Sojo, were said to have lived *tengu*, ruled over by an old king with white hair and a long, flowing beard. Yoshitsune's early lessons from *tengu* teachers are supposed to have resulted in an illustrious military career that continued until his thirty-second year, when, rather than face defeat at Takadachi, in modern-day Iwate Prefecture, he killed his wife and children, set his castle on fire, and committed suicide.

While *tengu* and demon quellers were imported, an entity uniquely native to Japan is the *kappa*. This curious creature has a beaked mouth, a scaly body covered by a tortoise shell, and a hollow on the crown of its head filled with a magical liquid from which it derives its strength and supernatural powers. *Kappa* can have quite evil intentions, luring children and washerwomen into the water and drowning them. To forestall *kappa* malevolence, however, one need only bow upon greeting it. Being Japanese, the *kappa* will immediately bow in return, thereby tipping out the magical fluid and rendering itself helpless. Or, one can try to tame a *kappa* by offering its favorite food, cucumber.

This unpredictable Japanese water spirit somewhat resembles one of the best-known ghostly beings of Scotland, the kelpie. Mostly haunting rivers, the kelpie lures the unwary to their death by drowning, usually by assuming the shape of a horse which invites its quarry to mount it, then plunges with its rider into the nearest stretch of water.

Animals, too, both real and mythical, play a vital role in the world of the Japanese supernatural. Creatures most likely to possess magical talents are foxes, badger-like animals called *tanuki,* and snakes. But the magician's parade also includes frogs, turtles, cats, dogs, monkeys, birds, mice, wolves, wild pigs, deer, horses, otters, weasels, spiders, butterflies, fireflies, and even lowly earthworms. Earthquakes in Japan, for instance, are believed to be caused when a gargantuan, subterranean catfish stirs in its sleep and sets the entire earth trembling. In tale and metaphor, animals are endowed with human characteristics, or vice versa. They frequently interact with human beings in mysterious ways, creating supernatural frameworks within which to tell stories, teach morals, or point out paths.

Foxes are preeminent tricksters, typically deploying their wiles to frighten, poke fun at, or sometimes seduce human beings. A fox can appear as a beautiful woman who bewitches a man into madness and death, or, more rarely, shows him gratitude for a kind deed he has done for her. The Japanese word for "fox," or *kitsune,* can even be used as an adjective for a particularly enchanting, attractive woman. At the same time, foxes have a charitable aspect: a fox is considered the messenger for the deity of abundant rice harvests, and pairs of foxes are evident throughout Japan as guardians at shrines to the god. Crafted of pottery, stone, or bronze, one of the pair carries in its mouth a jewel or power-granting scroll, while the other holds the key to a storehouse of wealth. A well-known fox tale dating back more than one thousand years tells of the "Golden Nine-tailed Fox," the female leader of a fox tribe who had caused considerable trouble in India and China. She escaped to Japan, and in a twelfth-century version assumes the guise of lady Tamamo no Mae. Loved by Emperor Toba (1103–56), she one day cast a spell on him, and he fell sick and almost died. She was eventually found out by the court astrologer, Abe no Yasunari, who held up a sacred mirror reflecting her true fox form. Pursued and cornered by a skilled archer, she transformed herself at the point of death into a rock that afterward was said to have killed instantly anyone foolish enough to touch its surface. The rock, dubbed *sessho seki,* or the "death stone," was finally destroyed in the fifteenth century by the holy monk, Genno, and stories say it disappeared with an enormous explosion of poisonous smoke.

Intriguingly, one report claims that the rock's supposed site in what is now Tochigi Prefecture contains unusually high levels of arsenic in the surrounding area.

Another wily schemer is the *tanuki,* and a legend from the Shojoji temple in Tatebayashi, Gunma Prefecture, tells of the lucky teakettle that was really a *tanuki,* leading the monks in a merry chase to capture it. When a *tanuki* reaches the age of one thousand years it acquires supernatural powers which enable it to transform its shape into all manner of living beings and objects, although its favorite disguise is a Buddhist priest. On a moonlit night a *tanuki* can lead travelers astray by beating on its enormous belly, emulating the comforting, rhythmic beat of a temple drum. Although they are more mischievous than truly evil, *tanuki* have been blamed for devouring the wives of woodcutters and accused of smothering hunters beneath their oversized scrota.

This pair of foxes acts as the twin guardians of a fox shrine.

Particularly strong mystic powers belong to snakes, which in ancient religions throughout the world have inspired reverential awe as well as fear. In Japan, a stylized snake dance, imported from India via China and Korea, used to be performed, reflecting an ages-old Japanese worship of snakes. A white snake is considered a messenger of the gods, while related serpent-dragons control water and weather and protect humankind from fire and pestilence. A Shinto ceremony at the Izumo Grand Shrine in Shimane Prefecture celebrates the arrival of Japanese deities riding on a great, white serpent. Old farmhouses in Japan often have a large snake, or *aodaisho,* slithering somewhere on the premises, and this is accepted as a good omen tied to the safety and fortune of the house and family. But lustful female snakes may seek human mates, transforming themselves into voluptuous women to seduce unsuspecting males. Snakes appear as symbols of fertility, untrammeled passion, and uncontrollable natural phenomena. One mythological interpretation depicts snakes as the connection between the world of mortals and the world of eternity.

Various specific properties are assigned to the astonishing array of animals on Japan's supernatural stage. Another messenger of the gods is the deer, a sacred animal associated with prosperity and longevity. Today, more than one thousand tame deer roam freely around the park in Nara, which served as the old capital city of Japan from 710 to 784. According to a much-loved Chinese legend adapted by the Japanese, a magical monkey king named Son Goku, along with a *kappa* and a boar, accompany the Buddhist priest Genjo Sanzo on his journey to India to collect sacred scriptures. Their travels are plagued by encounters with demons and ghosts, but the group eventually reaches India, where the priest studies at

Naranda Temple. After seventeen years, Genjo Sanzo returns to China bearing 657 volumes of sutras. He founds two new Buddhist sects and spends the rest of his life translating the holy texts he had gathered. Television viewers in Japan even now delight in the dazzling special effects that often accompany reenactments of this enduring story.

Additional imports from China include Japan's circle of mythical animals. The *nue* is a fabulous bird which has been variously described, with one version depicting it with the head of a monkey, the body of a *tanuki*, the paws of a tiger, and a tail that is a live snake. It was considered the evil spirit responsible for the illness of Emperor Konoe in 1153, and was shot down by the famous archer Minamoto no Yorimasa, then subsequently killed by one of the latter's retainers. Another composite animal is the *kirin*, which has the head of a dragon, the body of a deer, scales in place of hair, a strange, ridged breast, the tail of an ox, and the hooves of a goat. Although it runs faster than any other animal, its steps are soundless, and it never leaves any footprints behind. With a single, small horn that is fleshy, not hard, the *kirin* is regarded as a gentle creature without harmful intent to any living entity.

Such kindness is also a characteristic of the phoenix, the colorful cross between a peacock and a pheasant that was once adopted as the crest of the Japanese empress. The East Asian phoenix, unlike its Egyptian counterpart, is not reborn from its own ashes, but is very rare, appearing only once every thousand years. In 1052, Fujiwara no Yorimichi converted his second home in present-day Uji City, Kyoto, into what is now called the Byodoin temple, today used jointly by the Tendai and Jodo Buddhist sects. One elegant section is the Phoenix Pavilion, structured like a stylized phoenix, with two smaller phoenixes adorning the roof.

A ferocious *shishi* and her cub stand guard at the entrance to a shrine.

Standing at the entrance to many temples and shrines throughout Japan is the *shishi,* the conceptually misguided Chinese representation of a lion. In Korea the big cat was changed into the "Korean dog," but arriving in Japan it assumed a dual nature, the Korean dog and the Chinese lion, and some claim that it should technically be called a Buddhist lion. The *shishi* is distinguished by its large, squarish head, flat, broad nose, bulging eyes, and row of tight curls across its brow. In Buddhism, its primary task is the guardianship of temples and palaces, and, in this capacity, it is posted in pairs at entryways. The female lion often leans her paw on a cub, while the male has an open mouth, frequently holding a ball. The open and closed mouths utter, *"a"* and *"un,"* or the beginning and end of all creation, from the Sanskrit equivalent of alpha and omega.

The Chinese male principle of the universe is manifest in the dragon, which, as a rain deity associated with cosmic forces, exerts power over rain and storm. In Japanese art, dragons often do not appear fully visible and are usually depicted half-hidden by clouds or turbulent waves. This cautious approach may arise from the belief that mortals cannot gaze upon the entire body of a dragon and remain alive. A close relative of the snake, around which cult worship arose, dragons are described in Japan's earliest legends, yielding such treasures as "tide-ruling jewels" and a "herb-quelling sword."

Although animals are often endowed with human characteristics, once in a while the tables are turned. Human beings who behave in a beastly manner can be

The male *shishi* also stands guard at the shrine, on the opposite side of the entrance from the female.

changed into animals, as in the tale of an evil peasant in old Kyoto. The perpetrator of numerous foul deeds, he was finally transformed into a dog unable to eat, dying a miserable death after one hundred days. The monk Raigo, who lived during the tenth century, on the other hand, is said to have changed because of his inner furies into a monstrous rat which stole into the temple to tear up volumes of precious Buddhist sutras with his sharp, rodentine teeth. And humans can be reborn as serpents bent on revenge against those who wronged them in a former life.

Supernatural components also feature in the No plays traditionally enjoyed by the Japanese upper classes. There are ceremonial deities, pathetic warrior ghosts, and elegant female spirits. Kabuki, so enjoyed by the common people, also boasts a colorful repertoire of supernatural beings, especially male ghosts, although some renowned kabuki plays center on vengeful female ghosts. Japanese literature includes classic collections of ghost and monster stories, and, of course, the gods almost always play some part. Periods of sociopolitical turbulence in Japan's history were often marked by a resurgence of popular interest in the supernatural and the ghostly, perhaps underscoring the uncertainties of life and death during times of bewildering change.

Various manifestations of the supernatural strongly reemerged during Japan's Heian period (794–1185), as people sought to identify demons of disease and hunger, as well as beings able to transform their shapes and spirits of the dead. Over the next two hundred years, supernatural perceptions broadened to include human ghosts, as well as changeling animals, and during the Muromachi period (1392–1573), inanimate objects, too, were deemed powerful enough to change into living entities. In the

Momoyama era (1568–98) and the succeeding Edo era (1600–1867), however, interest in the supernatural significantly heightened, with ghost stories and other paranormal phenomena enthralling audiences. Edo-era artists, especially, were enamored of supernatural themes, creating forceful and detailed woodblock prints, hanging scrolls, and carved netsuke, to portray otherworldly scenes. Japan's deliberate push for Western-influenced modernization in the Meiji era (1867–1912) did not diminish popular fascination with the supernatural, which increasingly focused on human psychic powers and the strength of links between the living and hidden worlds.

A basis for the prevalence of the supernatural in Japanese culture and mores stems from the creation myth itself. Comparatively simplistic, the story of Japan's beginnings is chronicled in country's two earliest written histories, the *Kojiki,* or *Record of Ancient Matters,* set down in 712, and the *Nihon Shoki,* or *Chronicle of Japan,* compiled in 720. Combinations of legend, fact, and deliberate historical fabrication, these records are attempts to establish Japan's genealogical lineage and traditions.

Chronicles of the mythological Age of *Kami* set the Shinto pattern for everyday life and worship. The *Kojiki* tells of the *kami* of the Center of Heaven, which appeared first, followed by the *kami* of birth and growth. But actual creation begins with the brother-sister duo, Izanagi no Mikoto and Izanami no Mikoto, who descend from the High Plain of Heaven and give birth to everything, including other numerous *kami* and the Great Eight Islands, or Japan. Of the *kami* the three most important are Amaterasu the Sun Goddess, her obnoxiously behaved brother Susanoo no Mikoto, who governs the earth, and Tsukiyomi, the moon goddess in charge of the realms of darkness. Amaterasu, obviously a shaman warrior of superb magical powers, is the progenitor of Japan's main ruling families, and it is she who orders her grandson, Ninigi no Mikoto, to become the first actual ruler of Japan. As symbols of divine authority he receives a mirror, a sword, and a necklace of jewels, the three sacred treasures.

Given a historical background steeped in the supernatural, it small wonder that Japanese society offers an intriguing combination of the primitive and the sophisticated, the ancient and the trendy, the mystical and the mundane. This very balancing act epitomizes one dichotomy of Japanese culture itself, a persisting fact which dismays foreigners who wish that Japan would make up its mind over which face to show to the world. In this society of contrasts and contradictions, high technology seems melded with a high sense of supernatural possibilities. The company executive discussing international deals over his cellular telephone may seem up-to-the-minute and firmly grounded in Japan's technological present. In his inside pocket, however, he may well be carrying a magical charm to ward off bad fortune and evil spirits. The housewife whose home is filled with the latest electronic appliances may yet hang a protective amulet by her doorway to repel unwanted visitors come from the realm of ghosts and demons. Glass-and-steel skyscrapers symbolize Tokyo's thrust into an aggressively modern age, but from their ancient wooden shrines and temples, Shinto and Buddhist priests are still called upon to purify buildings and exorcise spirits of the restless dead.

As in other cultures, the supernatural in Japan provides a context in which to interpret the phenomenal world. It is both a way to explain the unexplainable and a means to attain deeper insight. As a spiritual quest for mystic seekers, it is a path to transcendence of human frailty and limitations. As folk belief in practice, such as the consecration of a shrine believed to be inhabited by unseen spirits, it is a framework for controlling or transmuting the mysteries of existence. In its present-day guise, it continues to function as a reminder that human beings are more than mere flesh and bones. Rather, humankind is a sentient, spiritual entity inextricably connected to a vast universe of unimaginable subtlety and richness that has yet to yield its secrets. Everywhere around us is magic, and the supernaturally magical event may await just around the next corner.

CHAPTER TWO

Psychic Stirrings

An important thread in Japan's supernatural tapestry is human psychic power. There have always been people able to enter another dimension of existence where "superpower" becomes possible. Japanese shamans called *miko*, for example, have long stood as agents between the ordinary world of human beings and the realms of the gods and the spirits. Traditionally unmarried women, *miko* communicate essential wisdom and exercise valuable healing gifts.

Their role was probably first defined during the

Age of *Kami*. The sun goddess Amaterasu had hidden herself in a celestial cave in disgust at the numerous outrages committed by her brother Susanoo. As a result, the heavens and earth had darkened. To cajole her into coming out again, the other *kami* arranged entertainment, and the heavenly shaman Ame no Uzume danced in front of the cave. Eventually Amaterasu emerged, and heaven and earth brightened once more.

In Japan's long history of shamanic and mediumistic practice, especially among religious groups, the ability to tap psychic potential has always played a part. It was not until about the mid-nineteenth century, however, that the paranormal phenomena taken for granted by members of such groups began to be investigated more objectively. Researchers started to examine Japanese people with supernatural powers in an attempt to illustrate and understand what was happening. At the same time, public interest was piqued by sensational press coverage of a number of colorful personalities. A variety of psychic abilities was showcased: clairvoyance, mediumship, telekinesis, and healing. There was sensation and secrecy, skepticism and suicide.

Among the early investigators was the Edo-era scholar Hirata Atsutane, whose specialty was Shinto, but who also looked into poltergeist and reincarnation. Another mystic researcher was Honda Chikaatsu, whose studies in meditation tied to divine possession led him to become a medium. His psychic training techniques were further developed within Omoto, a Shinto-related sect founded by the woman mystic Deguchi Nao in 1892, and whose members would themselves in turn establish various psychic and religious circles. In fact, beginning in 1814 and continuing for several decades afterward, there was a blossoming of religious movements which centered around faith healing, and became widely popular among Japan's peasant masses. A forerunner of these schools was the Kurozumi sect, which emphasized faith in the Sun Goddess, and was founded in 1814 by the Shinto priest Kurozumi Munetada. Kurozumi claimed mystical vision after recovering from a severe illness. The Tenri sect was started in 1838 by Nakayama Miki, a faith healer and wife of a farmer near Nara Prefecture. Still thriving today, it has established a major religious complex in Tenri City, Nara. Kawade Bunjiro, a farmer, established the Konko sect in 1859.

Deguchi Nao was born in the Kyoto Prefecture castle town of Fukuchiyama in 1836, during a period remembered as Tenpo no Daikikin, a time of famine and natural disaster, when several hundred thousand people died throughout Japan. Her family, Kirimura, had once been fairly well-to-do but had gradually become impoverished, and when she was ten years old, she was sent to work as a domestic servant. She returned home almost seven years later, and was then adopted into her aunt's family, Deguchi, in 1853. At the age of nineteen, she entered into a marriage that would last thirty-two years, until her husband's death in 1887. Five years later, in February 1892, she had her first religious vision when a god appeared to her and she began speaking aloud in a man's voice.

After several unsuccessful attempts at exorcism, she decided to accept her possession by a god she called Ushitora no Konjin, or the Golden God of the Northeast. After she was ordered by this god to undertake special training with water, her psychic powers developed rapidly, and she began engaging in healing, clairvoyance, and automatic writing. Prophesying—correctly, as it would turn out—Japan's war with China and then with Russia, she was arrested on April 21, 1893 on false charges, and after her release was held under house arrest for forty days.

Not interested in founding her own sect, she initially cooperated with the Konko sect, but when they ignored one of her automatic writing messages, she broke with them and erected a small shrine at her home in Ayabe, Kyoto. This act was considered unlawful by a government which had already begun to exercise strict control over religious activities and individuals with perceived special powers. By the time she died in 1918, at the age of eighty-one, Deguchi Nao, who had never attended school and who could not read or write, had produced one hundred thousand sheets (each about twenty-five by thirty-five centimeters) of automatic writing, which talked mainly of the need to change humankind and develop the three worlds of the phenomenal, the intimated, and the sacred. The sheets were made more legible by her son-in-law, Deguchi Onisaburo, who, with strong psychic strengths of his own, succeeded her as leader of Omoto.

Academic interest in the supernatural was evinced by Inoue Enryo, who in 1888 founded the Research Society for Supernatural Phenomena at Tokyo Imperial University (now Tokyo University). Around the same time, researchers at Meiji University began to introduce the results of Western psychic research to Japan. Books on psychic abilities were increasingly published.

One enthusiastic author and translator was Asano Wasaburo, the son of a doctor. Born in 1874, Asano studied English literature at Tokyo Imperial University, where he sat in on classes taught by Lafcadio Hearn. After graduation he became an English teacher at a naval school, building a career and reputation by writing many literary criticism papers. In 1915, however, he was so impressed by Omoto that he decided to give up teaching and join the sect full-time. Convinced that Deguchi's psychic gifts such as automatic writing were genuine, he published two books about the sect in 1921. Increasingly he came to believe in the power of spiritualism, and in 1923 he left Omoto to establish the Society for Psychic Science, with about twenty core members. Completely dedicated to the subject, he took part in the International Spiritualist Federation held in London, Great Britain, in 1928. The following year he founded the Tokyo Spiritualist Association, publishing a newsletter called *Spirit and Life,* and many related books.

Among the people who joined Asano's spiritualist studies in 1923 was Fukurai Tomokichi, perhaps the best known investigator of the psychic in Japan. He is especially remembered for his pioneering work in *nensha,* or thoughtography, the ability to psychically project thought images. Born in Takayama City, Gifu Prefecture in 1871, Fukurai studied psychology at Tokyo Imperial University, where he also taught after graduation, receiving a doctoral degree for his thesis on psychology and hypnosis. He married the daughter of a wealthy family, and his wife's constant financial support enabled him to pursue his passion for psychic research for the rest of his life.

In 1910 Fukurai Tomokichi began examining the clairvoyant Mifune Chizuko, the first time such testing had ever been tried in Japan. Born in 1886 in Kumamoto, on the island of Kyushu, Mifune was married in 1908 at the age of twenty-two to a military man who three weeks later was sent to Manchuria. In developing her clairvoyant gifts Mifune was aided by her brother-in-law, Kiyohara Takeo, who trained her in breathing and concentration. She was soon able to see through solid surfaces and to locate missing objects. As word spread, people began queuing outside her house to undergo psychic healing. Together Mifune and Kiyohara would accept three patients every morning; Mifune would look through the body and put her hand on the ailing or diseased part. Whenever she focused on the patient her hand would spontaneously tremble. Fukurai, who was to test her clairvoyant abilities on more than seventy separate occasions, considered her one of the world's greatest benefactors.

Pleased with the results of his observations, he arranged a five-day-long investigation together with a colleague from Kyoto University. Newspapers reported on the tests, and this press coverage inspired another clairvoyant, Nagao Ikuko, regarded as the first person in the world to demonstrate *nensha,* the projection of thought images onto undeveloped phtographic dry plates. Born into a high-class family in Yamaguchi Prefecture in 1871, she was seventeen when she married Nagao Yokichi, who became a judicial officer and finally a judge. After his retirement in Tokyo, the couple moved north to Tochigi Prefecture, and it was there that Nagao's clairvoyant powers became evident. When she was twenty, Nagao suffered the loss of her firstborn son, and she increasingly turned to inner faith to live. She became a devout worshipper of the Japanese sun goddess, Amaterasu Omikami, and would offer prayers every day for thirty minutes. When she read about Mifune in the newspapers, Nagao realized she had similar gifts; these were confirmed in experiments with Fukurai, who also recorded her *nensha* abilities.

In December 1910, that same year, Nagao, too, agreed to a series of experiments with *nensha:* Although avidly written about by the newspapers, the tests were ridiculed by scholars, especially physicists. Fukurai was denounced as a fraud; the ensuing controversy became such an embarrassment for the Japanese academic world that the leading physicist of the day, Yamakawa Kenjiro (also a former president of Tokyo University), decided to investigate personally.

The experiments began on January 8, 1911, but got off to a bad start when Yamakawa forgot to insert the dry plate at the right moment, resulting in Nagao's failure to accomplish *nensha*. The experiments were rescheduled, but public protest against this supernatural activity upset these plans. In addition, public opinion, fueled by media reporting, had turned against the two clairvoyants, who were widely perceived as frauds. In what would be her last experiment with Yamakawa, Mifune had inadvertently selected the wrong set of lead pipes to look through. Although she was successful with the pipes she used, the *Hochi* newspaper accused her of changing the pipes and of being nothing but a fraud. An accusation of fraud was also leveled at Nagao by the Osaka *Jijishinpo,* which ignored Yamakawa's demand for a retraction. Mifune's answer was to commit suicide on January 18, 1911, at the age of twenty-five. Next month, on February 26, the deeply discouraged Nagao, aged forty-one, also killed herself. Nor did the tragedy end there. Her husband, angered and demoralized, committed suicide one year later.

These events did not deter Fukurai, who began researching the clairvoyant Takahashi Sadako. In 1913 he published a book about the three women, entitled *Clairvoyance and Thoughtography.* In it, he stated that although "swarms" of scholars were against him, he knew that thoughtography and clairvoyance were facts. The result was an increased assault on his professionalism, which led to his resignation from Tokyo Imperial University. Writing that he had been expelled from the academic world, he voiced his loneliness as well as bewilderment at scholarly reaction to the observed facts in his experiments. Free of the university, he resolved to undergo spiritual training and so journeyed to sacred Mount Koya, in Wakayama Prefecture. He subsequently became a professor at the Buddhist Koyasan University, in 1926.

Still committed to psychic research, Fukurai started testing the *nensha* powers of Mita Koichi, who successfully projected a number of different images. The work

Strange things sometimes happen when taking photos at graves.

convinced Fukurai of the existence of a spirit world and in 1923 he published *Spirit and the Mysterious World,* in which he explained the psychic power behind *nensha* and clairvoyance. Along with Asano, he attended the International Spiritualist Federation in London, and three years later, in 1931, his *Clairvoyance and Thoughtography* was published in English, gaining him fame as the founder of *nensha.* Experiments in England with the psychic William Hope led Fukurai to believe that *nensha* and spiritual photography were essentially the same except that the former was due to human psychic ability while the latter came from another world.

Fukurai retired from Koyasan University in 1940 to devote himself full-time to psychic research. In 1945, he and his family were evacuated to Sendai, where he was made adviser to the Tohoku Psychic Research Society. He died in Sendai at the age of eighty-two.

Mita Koichi was born in Miyagi Prefecture in 1885, the second son of a samurai. From childhood, he had shown psychic abilities, especially clairvoyance, and was described by the family's Shinto priest as exceptionally pure-hearted and joyful. After a stint as a traveling salesman, at the age of twenty-three he founded a new religious sect, Seishin Shuyodan ("Spirit Training Group"), a name that was later changed to Teikoku Jikakukai ("Imperial Awakening Society"). Through this sect he traveled widely, exhibiting his psychic powers around Japan.

Hearing about Nagao Ikuko, he became intrigued by *nensha,* and experimented in it from 1914. On October 16, 1916, before an audience of some two thousand people gathered in Gifu Prefecture, Mita demonstrated *nensha* using various images suggested by spectators. Among the images projected onto the dry plate was a picture of nearby Ogaki Castle, as well as Japanese kanji characters. The following year, Mita and Fukurai met for the first time, after which Mita became an experimental medium. Dramatic tests were performed before crowds of 3,000 to 3,600 people, with Mita projecting well-known buildings, as well as an image of a former prime minister, Katsura Taro.

Because many people remained skeptical, Fukurai decided to have Mita project thoughts of unfamiliar images, so he selected the dark side of the moon. On June 24, 1931, at 8:20 A.M., Fukurai prepared two dry plates in a case at his house in Osaka. From his own house in Hyogo Prefecture, at 8:30 A.M., Mita thought-projected the images that Fukurai had requested. Fukurai immediately developed the plates and captured the transmitted images. Similar experiments were again carried out, this time in front of audiences, in 1933. There was no way at that time to check the validity of Mita's psychically projected images, but in 1959, the first space pictures of the dark side of the moon were taken. From 1969 to 1972 America's Apollo spacecraft also took numerous shots of the moon's dark side. Using these pictures, Dr. Goto Motoki, who served from 1960 to 1961 as president of the Agency of Industrial Science and Technology, confirmed the remarkable accuracy of Mita's images.

Mita demonstrated *nensha* numerous times, even for bureaucrats in Korea. During Japan's war with China he traveled to Manchuria in 1931 to do "dowsing" or locating water psychically. He was also involved in trying to locate sunken treasure. Although he, like Mifune and Nagao, was at times labeled a fraud, Mita fared much better than the two women. Becoming increasingly religious, he built a special altar in his house, an act which seemed to bring him good fortune. In 1943 he was named to the board of directors of an Osaka textile company, where he suddenly died of a stroke while talking with someone on the telephone. He was fifty-nine.

In 1946 the Japan Psychic Science Association was founded by scientists and mediums, and in 1952 the Fukurai Institute of Psychology was established. Around the same time, Motoyama Hiroshi founded the Institute for Religious Psychology to further investigate paranormal phenomena.

Although not tested by Fukurai, another contemporary of Mifune and Nagao was a woman named Chonan Toshie, who reportedly displayed remarkable supernatural abilities. Born in Yamagata Prefecture in 1863 to a samurai family, she became a domestic servant after her father died. She is believed to have vomited blood at the age of twenty-one and to have eaten less and less from the age of twenty-five. Despite this, she was incredibly strong, much stronger than even the male servants in the household, and she could effortlessly heft a barrel containing fifteen 1.8-liter bottles.

Chonan's spiritual powers became evident when she was thirty, when she began psychically locating missing objects. At the age of thirty-one she is said to have stopped passing stool or urine. Her stomach and chest swelled up for forty days, after which time she experienced divine possession and miraculous healing powers. As her fame grew, so did government suspicion of her activities, and when she was thirty-two, she was arrested and imprisoned for a period of sixty days. The following October she was reimprisoned for another seven days. Throughout these nine weeks, she supposedly passed no stool or urine. Although she had by then almost stopped eating entirely, she was force-fed about seventy-five grams of raw sweet potato every day.

Locked away by herself in a prison cell, she could nevertheless cause the materialization of various objects, including sacred water, talismans, medicines, and even sutras. Prison officials are said to have heard the sound of wind instruments playing whenever Chonan prayed, and although she could not bathe or wash, her hair and skin remained clean and sweet-smelling. After being freed from prison, Chonan continued to be visited by people eager to receive her materialized sacred water. Visitors would bring small, empty bottles, before which Chonan would pray. The bottles would spontaneously fill with a multicolored liquid. People then took the bottles away for use in healing, a purpose for which they were apparently extremely effective. Not everyone could receive the colored liquid, however. A bottle belonging to someone about to die (destined to die soon, Chonan would say) would not fill. Also remaining empty would be the bottle brought by someone who came merely to test whether Chonan was real or a fake. This miraculous materializing talent disappeared whenever anyone stood directly behind her. Until she died at the age of forty-four, Chonan was perceived as looking about half her age. Foretelling her own death by two months, she died in 1907.

Arrests and police surveillance of psychics and healers were common features of the Meiji period, which disliked ways of thinking which deviated from state-directed guidelines. Named for Emperor Meiji, this era in Japanese history is best remembered for its so-called Restoration in 1868, a concerted effort to completely restyle Japan by drawing on the technological expertise of the West. For more than two centuries immediately prior, Japan had been officially closed off from the rest of the world by the xenophobia of the Tokugawa shogunate. The country had experienced next to no contact with the

West or Western ideas, but the Meiji Restoration sought to reverse this situation. Western knowledge, notably in science, medicine, navigation, and gunnery, was rapidly assimilated into a society eager to enter a new era.

But such zealous embrace of the new meant that much of the old was discarded. Supernatural activities were particularly suspect. In 1873, for example, a law was passed forbidding mediums and psychics to practice their powers. The following year another law made it illegal for faith healers and psychic healers to contradict acceptable medical practice by offering healing alternatives. Actually, medicine itself experienced a major upheaval at this time. For 1,500 years, *kanpo*, or Japanese herbal medicine in the Chinese tradition, had prevailed as the orthodox system of medicine in Japan. With the Meiji Restoration's drive to catch up with the West, however, *kanpo*, despite its long history and proven clinical performance, was suddenly dismissed as unsophisticated and unscientific compared with such Western disciplines as anatomy and surgery. In 1875, in a move that almost destroyed traditional medicine in Japan, the Meiji government restricted the official licensing examination for all physicians to Western medicine. From 1906, only doctors thus licensed were permitted to prescribe *kanpo*. In 1882, another law stipulated that only patients already under a doctor's care could even go to receive psychic healing.

Religion, too, was overhauled. Two of the main objectives of the Restoration of 1868 were to restore the emperor to direct rule, and to create a common spiritual basis for society and government. For centuries Shinto, a *kami*-centered faith, had been a communal form of worship intimately associated with daily life. It had no written creed that served as a religious guide, but shrines (the Japanese name for which is *jinja*, meaning "*kami* dwellings") were places where sacred spirits could be invited so that human beings could easily experience their presence. Dating from Japan's prehistory, such shrines were tied to communities all over the country. The Meiji reforms drastically changed this focus.

Shrine Shinto, a native way of thinking spiritually, was replaced with "State Shinto," a nationalized religion that made shrines state institutions and shrine priests government officials. The Meiji organization of a shrine system

A sense of the sacredness of a place pervades Japan's supernatural world.

greatly reduced the number of shrines, which at the beginning of the twentieth century numbered almost two hundred thousand. Permitted shrines were assigned grades in 1871 according to their ties to the Imperial Family, hereditary priesthood was abolished, and the government took over title to all shrine property, often selling off land. There was also an official but ultimately unsuccessful attempt to suppress Buddhism, which was seen as detracting from Shinto as the state cult.

On April 25, 1869, Emperor Meiji signaled the indivisibility of throne and Shinto by conducting a Shinto ceremony, and in 1875 the government even prepared standard prayers which were required to be used in the rites of all shrines. Until then, individual priests had composed prayers as they saw fit at each shrine. During World War II the nationalistic character of Shinto was intensified to suit military ends, but on December 15, 1945, after Japan's defeat, the Allied Powers ordered a separation between shrine and state. From then, shrines once again became private, spiritual institutions supported by their local communities.

The establishment of a state cult meant, of course, that cults functioning outside of official sanction were considered a threat. The Omoto sect, which since its founding had grown large and powerful, perhaps inevitably became the target of unusually severe government persecution. In 1921 authorities imprisoned Deguchi Onisaburo and destroyed Omoto's shrine at Ayabe. After his acquittal in 1927, he built a new shrine at Kameoka, Kyoto, which did little to calm government suspicion. On December 8, 1935, in a raid at 4 A.M., some 430 police surrounded Omoto's facilities at Ayabe and Kameoka. They used the pretext that Omoto had armed itself with pistols and its young male members were trained to fight.

Deguchi Onisaburo, then sixty-four years old, was rearrested and imprisoned, along with his son, and both were badly tortured. Police reports to the print media portrayed the cult as demonic, mysterious, and strange, and authorities publicly vowed that the leader would be executed or imprisoned for life. The police even went so far as to set up sex-related materials in Deguchi Onisaburo's private rooms, and the media were then invited in to photograph this "evidence" of the suspicious cult leader's "woman problems." Karasawa Toshiki, the police chief, revealed the government's intent to "rid the earth of the Omoto sect."

The government subsequently prosecuted sixty-one key Omoto leaders, all of whom were convicted for disturbing the public peace. Authorities then dynamited the sect's facilities, with the damage so severe that the fires burned for over a month. They also dug up the grave of Deguchi Nao, destroying not only her tomb, but also all of the surrounding trees. Her remains were then moved to the corner of a public cemetery and given a cheap wooden marker. The Deguchi family tomb was also desecrated, as was the charnel house for Omoto followers. Still more, the symbol of the Omoto sect was erased from all headstones where it was displayed.

In September 1945, Deguchi Onisaburo was again acquitted and released, and in February the following year he restarted Omoto under the name Aizenen. He died on January 19, 1948, at the age of seventy-six. The Omoto sect still exists today.

Like so many eccentrics in the world of Japan's supernatural, Chonan and the Deguchis reflect a long lineage of mystics and psychics, each claiming or demonstrating unique gifts. Tanaka Morihei (1882–1928), for example, felt he could see through bodies and heal disease. In 1911 he showed his psychic powers in China and Mongolia, where he announced he was a human deity. Controlling mind and spirit through the practice of *reishi,* the flamboyant Tanaka engaged in a wide variety of activities, including standing for the House of Representatives, founding a healing clinic, and quarreling with the Omoto sect.

Another controversial figure was Hamaguchi Yugaku (1878–1943), a healer who treated patients by slicing his hands in the air. His therapy must have been effective, because even journalists and police detectives became his patients, along with members of the aristocracy. In 1926 he traveled to America to show his powers and compete as a magician. He won, garnering a considerable sum of prize money. Regarded as strange and even somewhat retarded in his childhood, Hamaguchi told fortunes and trained as a monk. As an adult he married four times, and had numerous mistresses. In his huge house he would host almost nightly saké parties, ostensibly to dispel the sadness he always felt. As his healing fame spread, people waited day and night outside his front door to see him, but police, spurred by a nervous Meiji government that frowned on potentially disruptive psychic activities, arrested him countless times. He was usually released because his activity was argued to be spiritual rather than medical.

A much quieter sort was Kuwahara Tennen, (1873–1906). A former teacher who had taught himself hypnotism from books, Kuwahara eventually wrote a best-selling book on mystical practice. Born in Gifu Prefecture, in 1903 he moved to Tokyo, where he continued to develop his mental and spiritual powers. As a healer he sucked up phlegm and pus from sick patients—even those with tuberculosis—with his mouth, calling his psychic healing power "benevolence." He later died of tuberculosis.

Such phenomena, eagerly covered by the print media, ensured that Japanese interest in the supernatural would remain strong, even in defiance of government disapproval. In 1930, for example, there were some thirty thousand known psychic healers throughout Japan. Understandably, most patients simply sought easy cures, with little or no deep interest in the supernatural or psychic powers. But at the same time there was a veritable boom in paranormal training and display, as growing numbers of more curious people sought to explore the unexplainable for themselves. Buddhism had long taught the importance of the "sixth sense," or the minds of the conscious and subconscious, and mystic seekers sought to further explore this, as well as the dimensions of the seventh and eight senses. Here, the supernatural was no longer "super," but normal and accessible. People with obvious psychic gifts were often regarded as pointers along the mystic path by those committed enough to undertake the arduous journey.

Research, both individual and institutional, continued after the Second World War. Several new organizations were founded, including the Japan Society for Parapsychology, the Japan Association for Psychotronic Research, and the Japan *Nengurafii* Association. *Nengurafii,* or metal-bending ability, was claimed by the teenager Kiyota Masuaki, who was touted as the Japanese Uri Geller, and extensive experiments with him were carried out in 1977. Several of these tests were filmed for American television in "Exploring the Unknown," a ninety-minute program aired by the National Broadcasting Company on October 30, 1977.

The stage for present-day supernatural investigations had been firmly set.

CHAPTER THREE

New Forays into the Mystic

The small room at Nippon Medical School is an unlikely setting for Zen meditation, but Sato Daishin, a Rinzai sect Buddhist, does not seem to mind. Arranging his simple monk's robe, he settles himself comfortably on the cushion to prepare himself for sitting meditation, or *zazen*. Round about him on the floor is a mess of coaxial cables, which are also attached to an antenna positioned two meters behind him. No cables touch the monk, but the antenna will nevertheless pick up his body's electromagnetic field. To protect against interference, the four walls and ceiling have been shielded with a fine metal mesh curtain.

As Sato Daishin begins his forty-five-minute meditation, Nomura Harehiko, the physicist who invented the antenna, and Kawano Kimiko, a physicist at Nippon Medical School, begin the measurement. The monk's breathing slows to about three breaths per minute, with the outbreath as long as twenty-five to twenty-eight seconds. The room becomes stiflingly hot, and halfway through the meditation the monk's concentration breaks, but is expertly recovered. Later, the antenna readings are plotted according to Fourier analysis, which determines the harmonic components of a complex waveform. The conclusion drawn from the sharp spikes on the graph is that as he meditates, the monk naturally emits *ki*.

For Nomura and Kawano, once again the mystic practice of meditation has successfully met modern science in this experiment designed to research and measure *ki*, the Japanese pronunciation of the Chinese character *chi*, or *qi*. No discussion of spiritual or supernatural energies in Japan is possible without mentioning *ki*, an ancient metaphysical principle integral to Oriental philosophy. Never clearly defined, even in Asia, *ki* is difficult to translate directly, but can be understood as the fundamental creative energy which permeates all things. There is the *ki* of the universe, as well as individual *ki*, usually manifested in breath power. *Ki* practitioners believe that at the core of every human being lies this world-forming energy waiting to be individually awakened.

Ki has more than four thousand years of history in China, where it is also expressed in the form of yin-yang dualism. From this arose the Chinese Five Elements Theory and the *Book of Changes*, or *I-Ching*, probably the first book to teach the Chinese people about the variations of *ki* in nature and humans. In India *ki* was known as *prana;* the ancient Greeks called it *pneuma.* Today, training in so-called internal *ki ko* (*qi gong* in Chinese) is concerned with personal health improvement and heightened spiritual development. External *ki ko,* on the other hand, is often used as a form of psychic healing, and can be an effective martial art.

Experiments in the physical measurement of *ki* have been a consuming interest of Nomura Harehiko for the last seven or so years. Officially the senior researcher in the superconductor application lab at MITI's electrotechnical laboratory at Tsukuba Science City, Nomura is also an inventor who has studied at America's M.I.T. Describing himself as a "professional of *ki,*" he conducts numerous experiments into its physical nature. He is also a founding member of the Mind Body Society, a group of some eight hundred members drawn from a wide variety of scientific disciplines, but which has also attracted mystics and philosophers. Founded in 1990, the society holds annual meetings which witness the results of its latest scientific research, including exploration of the supernatural.

Nomura explains that the human body is a wave emitter and that actually all living things emit and receive electromagnetic waves through the skin, an organ which once played a much more vital role in communication than it does now. Telepathy, for example, may have been an everyday, ancient ability, the art of which gradually disappeared through the centuries. Because an electromagnetic wave is very complex, Nomura measures what he calls the "power average" emitted from meditating monks. Emission of *ki* as evidenced by the sharp spikes is extremely important in *ki* practice. Nomura points out that the spike can be negative, at which time it is taking in energy because the monk is absorbing energy, or healing himself. A positive spike shows that the monk is emitting *ki* or releasing energy, which means that he is potentially healing others.

Some *ki ko* practitioners believe that the ancient practice of healing by laying on of hands is most likely a subtle form of electrical stimulation. The human body is made up of numerous and varying electrically conductive materials, which create a living electromagnetic field and circuit. Electromagnetic energy is being continuously generated in the human body through normal biochemical processes, as well as by the electromagnetic forces deep within the cells. In addition, human beings are being constantly affected by external electromagnetic fields arising from the earth below and the sky above.

In fact, every cell of the human body functions like an electric battery able to store electric charges. Actually, the human body is like a huge battery assembled from millions and millions of tiny batteries. All these batteries together constitute the human electromagnetic field. Each body cell can function like a miniature radio receiver, with a characteristic, measurable frequency. Before the cell can receive other frequencies, it requires an electric potential (voltage), which it draws from the water that constitutes about sixty to sixty-five percent of the adult human body. The human body seems specifically designed to receive fundamental energies in the form of vibrations from its surroundings.

Despite its long history in East Asia, *ki* has only in the last century become a legitimate topic of research at Japanese universities and scientific institutions. Trailblazers include Motoyama Hiroshi, with his work in the paranormal as well as *ki*. Using a technique known as meridian measurement, Motoyama used electrodes strategically placed on the fingers to send voltage pulses which demonstrate the path of internal *ki*. Machi Yoshio, of Tokyo Denki University, is well known for his measurement of internal *ki* as it relates to brain waves. A close friend and sometime research associate of Nomura, Machi believes that *ki* may have properties similar to a wave, and that it may be emitted from and received by special points in the body known as *tsubo* in acupuncture. Recent research has shown that the conductivity of the skin is much higher at these acupuncture cavities, which can be pinpointed precisely simply by measuring the skin's conductivity. Today, guided by Machi, Tokyo Denki University researchers are continuing investigations of *ki* emissions, while at Tohoku Technology University *ki ko* practitioners have been found to be able to control their movement of *ki,* an ability that manifests itself through such acts as emitting light from the center of the forehead, the same area marked by a crystal in ancient statues of Buddha.

For those who want to see *ki* power in action, an exciting display is routinely staged by Nishino Kozo, founder of the Nishino Ballet Group, in Shibuya. Now sixty-eight years old, Nishino was fifty when he started studying the martial arts of *kenpo,* or Japanese fencing, and aikido, which means the "way" *(do)* of "harmony" *(ai)* with *ki.* He rapidly developed a breathing technique meant to harness and circulate internal *ki,* and each week, several hundred students are, one by one, tossed or sent somersaulting about the room by Nishino's seemingly effortless use of *ki.*

Typically thrown back and upward onto a large, soft wall, students scream, giggle, twist, turn, and tumble, all the while apologizing or saying thank you. Even those in their seventies and eighties seem to have bodies which have suddenly turned into rubber. Some flip over and bounce down on their heads. Others roll off into the corner and have to be stopped by waiting assistant instructors. Successfully catering to a burgeoning public interest in perceived *ki* power, Nishino boasts a considerable following that includes several company presidents, as well as doctors, university professors, monks, martial artists, students, and the elderly. He now has twenty-eight assistant instructors, all of whom wear the uniform of a white polo shirt and dark pants.

Nishino, who had planned to be a doctor but gave up medical studies at the age of twenty-two to become a ballet dancer, believes that the energy of *ki* is fundamental. In fact, he is convinced that *ki* is a form of communication that takes place at the level of the body's DNA. He hypothesizes the existence of what he calls a "biospark," a spark of energy—*ki*—inside the cell. According to Nishino, a protein promoter releases the potential of the biospark, and this promoter can be stimulated through breathing techniques and *ki* training. The everyday breathing pattern of the majority of people is extremely shallow, but it can be changed so as to affect the body's cells more deeply. Nishino explains that students seem so happy when they receive *ki* because communication with the body's deeper internal level is very joyful for the cells, which experience a heightened energy exchange. A flamboyant, visibly energetic man, Nishino also claims his *ki* is so strong that it can change the color of diamonds.

In mainland China, training techniques were kept secret until the last twenty years, but instructors are now flocking to Japan to meet a booming interest in such *ki*-related arts as *taikyokuken* (*taijiquan* in Chinese) and *ki*-based healing therapy. The Chinese have long believed that human life depends upon proper circulation of *ki* in the body, and that stagnant or stopped-up *ki* leads to illness. *Ki ko* practitioners can train their *ki* to circulate more smoothly, and can also let it flow to help others. To this end training encompasses both internal and external exercises, usually through meditation and specialized physical movements.

There are three main types of *ki*. Heaven *ki* comprises the forces exerted upon the earth by the sun, the moon, the stars, and the planets, and as such it controls weather, climate, and natural disasters. Rainstorms and tornadoes are a way for Heaven *ki* to recover its energy balance, which must be maintained. Located beneath Heaven *ki* is earth *ki*, which is made up of lines and patterns of energy across the earth's surface, as well as the strong heat hidden in the earth's core. Earthquakes are also a means of recovering essential energy balance. The third type of *ki* exists within each individual person, animal, and plant. When this personal *ki* field is out of alignment, living beings grow sick and die, eventually decomposing.

Despite these seemingly clear-cut classifications, the East Asian definition of *ki* is actually quite broad, and *ki* can be generally defined as any type of energy that shows strength and power, including light, heat, magnetism, and electricity. Different energy states can also be called *ki*.

Well-attended classes on releasing *ki* potential are taught by Kurita Masahiro, a former Buddhist priest who is now a physician on the Faculty of Medicine at Tokyo University. The author of more than seventeen books, Kurita regularly appears on television to showcase his *ki*-related finger rotation exercises and super reading skills. Kurita, who undertook mystic training for more than nine years, sees *ki* as a type of information connecting body and mind; one that can dramatically change our lives. If one can hear music, Kurita assures us, then one can also learn to hear the vibration inherent in all things, including plants, the earth, and even the sun, moon, and stars. He believes that such abilities, usually seen as supernatural, or as a type of "superpower," are not super at all, but normal, and that human beings need only train to awaken such latent, inherent talents.

MITI allocated government funds to undertake a preliminary look into the paranormal and such topics as *ki* in a "sensitivity study" begun in October 1992 and completed in May 1993. The report's preliminary conclusion was that Japan ought to begin integrating existing knowledge from diverse fields to create a fusion of information that will shape future scientific research. The long-term objective, of course, is to better understand such phenomena as the "sixth sense" and the mechanism behind *ki* power, as well as telepathy, various psychic abilities, and even the mystical experience.

Within MITI there has been an informal study group dedicated to exploring the supernatural. Every month the group receives some sort of demonstration or lecture in supernatural powers. Guests have included Uri Geller, the controversial Israeli psychic best known for his spoon-bending feats, as well as Chinese *ki* practitioners. Even Asahara Shoko, the leader of AUM Supreme Truth, the doomsday cult that achieved notoriety after nerve gas attacks attributed to it in 1994 and 1995, was scheduled to show his levitation talents. The former head of this MITI study group, Hashimoto Hayashi, who now teaches at Saitama University, believes that rational, scientific methods can be used to explain what is currently viewed as irrational and inexplicable.

By combining high technology with more esoteric energies, Japanese researchers may eventually be able to create different models for perceiving both the phenomenal and supernatural worlds. One recent theory supposes the existence of a "neuron modulator," akin to a spiritual "field" running through nerves—a biological counterpart to the field theory of the new physics. Development of such theories may mean that the phenomenon of "sixth sense" will soon be explainable scientifically. Some MITI researchers are hopeful that the traditional, static models long used to explain the universe will be replaced by dynamic models that perceive things in a new way. Inomata Shuichi, who was the chief researcher at MITI's electrotechnical laboratory, hypothesized that *ki* is akin to a neutrino, an elementary particle at the level of the conscious mind. A founder of Japan Conscience Engineering, Inomata has proposed a mathematical transformation formula based on Einstein's principle $E=MC^2$ to illustrate the existence of *ki*.

Social scientists have noted that the collapse of the so-called bubble economy of the mid-1980s is prompting renewed awareness of considerations beyond the material world. Increasing numbers of Japanese are openly questioning what life is all about. Beneath the glitter of economic prosperity is stirring an individual search for deeper meaning that may well come to include the supernatural. This explains, in part, the current enthusiasm for joining new religious groups. Notwithstanding negative publicity over AUM Supreme Truth, religion thrives in Japan, a nation with a long history of sects and fringe cults. Many sects have taken a cue from Omoto, with former members leaving to set up splinter groups. And although women have typically been accorded a more lowly status than men in modern Japanese society, they have played key roles in cults through the ages, with female mystics often being the founders of new organizations. Their intuition and shamanic gifts have been recognized and valued, and women have many times been seen as having easier access to the realm of the supernatural.

In Japan today there are 183,996 religious groups recognized by the government, and another 47,023 without such recognition. Each has its own creed and philosophy. Of course, the current numbers are due less to supernatural leanings and more to the Religious Corporation Law, which was enacted in 1947 and replaced the Peace Preservation Law, which had imposed much stricter control over beliefs, activities, and groups deemed threatening to Japan's prewar and wartime governments (hence the suppression of Omoto). The Religious Corporation Law provides outstandingly attractive privileges, including tax reductions in thirty-three different businesses, including bathhouses, hair salons, entertainment operations, real estate, inns and restaurants, and medical institutions. Temple admission fees and sales of temple talismans and charms are tax-exempt. Once a religious group is officially recognized, Japanese law currently bars authorities from reexamining its activities, a precaution designed to protect religious freedom.

The founding of Omoto represented a second wave in the movement to establish non-traditional religious groups in Japan. Between 1892 and 1938, seven new groups—the "new religions"—were formed. By far the largest of these new religions is Soka Gakkai, a lay Buddhist group founded in 1930, and boasting an estimated eight million families of believers throughout Japan. Powerful enough to control a significant part of Japan's legislative apparatus, Soka Gakkai has been criticized for wielding too much influence, especially among Japan's decision makers. Internally, followers have raised the current leader, Ikeda Daisaku, to the level of monarch.

A third wave began in 1948, and from then until 1987

another eight groups were founded, known as "new, new religions." One of these, Kofuku no Kagaku, or the Science of Happiness, was founded in 1986 and claims five million loyal believers. AUM Supreme Truth was established in 1987 and grew to around ten thousand members in Japan (with several more tens of thousands overseas, notably in Russia).

Secret traditions have always had strong appeal, particularly among the more mystically inclined sects. Much

This torii marks the entrance to a Shinto shrine.

of such secrecy concerns the development of supernatural powers, namely the psychic abilities that will lead devotees to a higher spiritual path. Thus, followers of the
Tendai Buddhist sect undertake an arduous thousand-
day training course at Kyoto's Mount Hiei, and members
of the Shingon Buddhist sect complete physically pun-
ishing practices at in Wakayama's Mount Koya. The aus-
terity of Zen Buddhism is by now very familiar to many
foreigners intrigued by East Asian mystic thought. Zen
breathing techniques, which are typically necessary for
dedicated meditation, can lead to a transformation within the body that many practitioners consider divine.

One Japanese mystic—also known for his impressive
golf swing—is Masaki Kazumi, now based in a private laboratory in Okayama. This eighty-year-old dabbler in the
fantastic and mystical is a prolific inventor credited with
originating as many as 960 inventions, among them the
electric rice cooker, the electric guitar, a lie-detector
machine, moving stage lights, radar for fishing use, electric massage machines, and the "Biolite," a special type of
task lighting that significantly diminishes eye strain.

Many bizarre and unexplainable happenings sur-
round this soft-spoken, yet energetic man. In October
1976, for example, he claims a pearl suddenly popped
from his mouth. Originally 3.85 millimeters in diameter,
it grew to thirteen millimeters and has been expertly valued at eight million yen. The pearl shrinks whenever he
feels unwell. Another time, a woodlike statue materialized and spontaneously formed into a likeness of the Japanese god Daikoku, an experience he wrote about in his
book *I Saw a Miracle*. When the composition of the statue
was analyzed, it was determined to be a material unknown
on earth. The statue and pearl are only two of many such
apparitions. He also had a bottle of saké which provided

alcohol endlessly for more than one and a half years without running out. Some visitors to his research laboratory receive bookmarks fashioned from four-leaf clovers. These clovers are said to have spontaneously changed their form from three leaves into four over a period of a few days, in response to Masaki's specific request that they do so. A firm believer in past lives, Masaki recalls his former existences, one of which was as a Nichiren priest eight hundred years ago, when he wrote Buddhist sutras. He also dashed off a piano composition which he performed in Tokyo, although he has never studied piano. He believes the music came from a past life as a musician.

Masaki states that almost every human has two souls. The first soul comes into existence in the womb just before the mother becomes pregnant. This first life contains all knowledge about former lives, including character, work, and relationships; one's encounters in this life, whether positive or negative, are deeply connected to one's past. When the child is about eleven years old, the second soul usually enters, and that soul determines what sort of person one will be in this life. Using a pendulum, Masaki determines a visitor's human nature by analyzing what he calls the *fuchi* pattern cast by the pendulum on a sheet of blank paper. He says that on March 7, 1973, a voice came to him while he was on the campus of Osaka University, ordering him to make a pendulum using a bar magnet. At first he did not know how to use it, but accidentally discovered that it moved in a certain way when held over his arm. He tested others and found different movement patterns, so over the next three months he further tested three hundred people. By 1993 he had examined thirty thousand people. As a result, Masaki claims to be able to pinpoint intelligence level exactly, as well as basic nature and human potential. When he begins to use the pendulum, suspended from a copper wire, he first clears his mind. Soon he sees a white or gold light emanating from the magnet, and senses a shock to his chest. After that the magnet begins to move. He feels confident that he can predict at what age someone will die, although he only releases this information if he thinks the person concerned has the ability to change some aspect that will postpone the date of death. Masaki knew his own life would end at the end of January 1979, so when he was told in 1978 that he needed dental work, he refused, saying that he was going to die very soon. On New Year's Day of 1979, however, he was at home when he heard a deep voice booming. The voice explained it belonged to one Hachiman Daibosatsu, Masaki's guardian, and that it was going to grant him an extended life span and many supernatural powers as a reward for Masaki's contributions to humankind.

Born in Hyogo Prefecture in 1916, Masaki started doing breathing exercises when he was six years old, inhaling for seven seconds and exhaling for seven seconds for one hour each night. After three years of such practice he says he received clairvoyant powers and his brain waves reached theta level. When he was in the third grade of elementary school he explained the Nichiren Buddhist sutras to his mother. From a very early age, therefore, he was aware of his spiritual capabilities and the importance of the supernatural. Masaki attended Osaka Imperial University (now Osaka University), where he studied aeronautical and other engineering fields. As a student he began inventing numerous gadgets, and during World War II was nominated by other researchers as the person best able to begin to develop a new weapon. After World War II, at the medical department of Osaka University, he conducted research into the nervous system and invented low-frequency-based medical equipment. He also served as head of the Craft Center in the university's engineering department. Among his many contributions is his unique way of hitting the ball in golf. His method, which entails coordinating the body's center of gravity with how the club is gripped, enables him to consistently hit 340 or so yards, and he has trained Japanese professional golfers.

Masaki believes the mind can accomplish anything it wants to do, providing will and training are sufficient. The mind's capacity is unlimited and supernatural powers are available to anyone who wants them. One of his more recent inventions is his "Para Memory II Brain Potentialriser," which looks like a Sony Walkman, complete with earphones. Meant to enhance brain function, the small machine uses a range of sounds to influence brain wave frequencies. Anyone who can reach theta wave level frequency, for example, can allegedly bend spoons without effort. After watching a television program about Uri Geller in 1973, Masaki invented a machine to examine metal stress, which he tested using mental power. He concludes that mental power alone can create stress in metal. In November 1974 Masaki tossed a spoon into the air, where it snapped in two. After being examined more closely, the spoon split again. An elementary school boy whom he tested tossed up a blank sheet of paper and crayons into the air and a picture was instantly drawn on the paper. Masaki also tested and observed the ability to move and manipulate solid materials easily, such as bending metal through mental effort alone, even from several hundred meters away.

Masaki has personally experienced and documented at least twenty-three different supernatural or psychic phenomena, including an out-of-body journey in Naga-

no Prefecture in 1975. He also believes that he and another psychic, Miho, were friends in Atlantis some 120
million years ago. One piano composition is supposedly
healing music from Atlantis, and Masaki has used it for
patients suffering from mental depression.

Curing people has become the focus of the Hokkaido
healer known as Akutsu. A former veterinarian, Akutsu
heals by thumping people expertly and yelling. He, too,
has a significant following, and his healing powers have
been observed and measured by Nomura Harehiko. In
1994 Nomura and Machi tested Akutsu in Machi's laboratory at Tokyo Denki University. A practicing Christian,
Akutsu makes the sign of the cross before starting treatment, which usually consists of hitting the patient's back-
bone. Nomura used his antenna to register changes from
the patient's palm before and during Akutsu's emission
of *ki*, which he sends via his hands or eyes. The patient's
feet were also tested during treatment, to see whether
there were corresponding changes in their internal *ki*.

Another healer quietly working in Japan today is
Takahata Hikaru, who was a white-collar worker in a
Japanese company when he inadvertently discovered his
healing gifts. When a close family member fell seriously
ill, Takahata was able to use his hands to heal the patient.
Now retired from his company, he has since healed thousands of people, and his transformed life was recently
made into a movie.

Psychic power also involves the ability to harness
nature's awesome power. In Japan, one way of achieving
this is through the help of *fusui*, the Japanese reading of
the Chinese term *feng shui*, meaning "wind and water."
Fusui is the ancient East Asian practice of geomancy, a
complicated system of divination used to select the most
auspicious site for a grave or house and determine how it

should be constructed. Such divination insures that inhabitants benefit from harmonization with the surrounding environment, the basic principle being that humans should not disrupt existing natural order by indiscriminately modifying the landscape. After careful siting, architectural design is expected to go beyond requirements of space, form, and structure, to express more deeply a balance with the physical environment. *Fusui* practitioners believe the system can harness vital *ki,* thereby ensuring continuing prosperity for themselves and for future generations.

Inventors of the south-pointing compass, ancient Chinese thought they had discovered a vast magnetic field enveloping the earth. In fact, constantly traveling between the north and south poles were subtle forces, both electromagnetic and psychic. Dragons or serpents were believed to best exemplify these undulating energy rhythms, so the paths along which such forces move became known as "dragon paths," the basis for wind and water theory. Dragon paths are loosely analogous to electrical current running through a cord, with access to the current represented by the socket, or *ketsu,* in Japanese. This is the point at which *ki* can be harnessed in *fusui*. Access to vital energy through proximity to a *ketsu* makes some places much more auspicious than others. The quality of a place may also be judged by assessing three important geomantic criteria: mountains, watercourses, and directions. The central idea is to calm wind and acquire water.

Japan reportedly has many *ketsu*. One such energy outlet in Tokyo is the site of Edo Castle, now the Imperial Palace. Another is the thickly wooded Meiji Shrine, a Shinto sanctuary dedicated to Emperor Meiji and his consort. Indeed shrines throughout Japan may have been constructed on *ketsu* locations, showing that the ancient

Japanese, like other peoples, may have been extremely sensitive to the earth's energy fields, locating shrines where they most strongly experienced a feeling of power. Such sites include Chichibu in Saitama Prefecture, Hakone in Kanagawa Prefecture, Ise in Mie Prefecture, Miwa in Nara Prefecture, and Atsuta in the city of Nagoya. *Ketsu* mountains include Mount Fuji, which is said to radiate power in several directions, and sacred Mount Osore.

The Fujiwara family, which dominated northern Tohoku through four successive generations and also established the ancient capitals of Nara and Kyoto, were particularly noteworthy devotees of *fusui,* which they seriously studied and applied, even sending a son to learn the science in China during the seventh century. The first head of the Fujiwara dynasty was originally buried in Osaka, but his sons moved the body to Nara because *fusui* decreed this to be a much more auspicious location for positively influencing his offspring. In fact, as recently as the 1990s, some Japanese credited Hosokawa Morihiro's good fortune in becoming prime minister to the fact that he is directly descended from the Fujiwara family, of which Hosokawa's maternal grandfather, former prime minister Konoe Fumimaro, was also a scion.

Nor was the fact that the influence of *fusui* is believed to extend through the centuries lost on Tokugawa Ieyasu (1542–1616), the charismatic shogun who founded the Tokugawa shogunate at present-day Tokyo. So convinced was he of *fusui's* efficacy that he is said to have hoarded all available knowledge of it for exclusive use by himself and his family, effectively making *fusui* secret in Japan. Acting according to *fusui* principles, Tokugawa went so far as to relocate the burial sites of his rivals, supposedly to ensure that powerful grave energies could not extend to their descendants.

In addition to placing Edo Castle on a *ketsu,* Tokugawa left detailed instructions on how his funeral and burial should be handled to project his influence into future generations, leaving none of his heirs' affairs to chance. Eventually he was buried at the Toshogu Shrine in Nikko, a grandiose mausoleum built by some fifteen thousand artisans laboring for two years at his grandson Iemitsu's command. Constructed according to *fusui* guidelines, Toshogu and the neighboring Futarasan Shrine are thought to receive positive energy generated by the nearby sacred mountain, Mount Nantai.

From its beginnings *fusui* has been inseparable from yin-yang dualism and the Five Elements Theory, the Chinese doctrine that all things and events are products of yin (the vital energy of the earth) and yang (the vital energy of the heavens). Yang interacts with yin to produce the five elements, or agents: metal, water, wood, fire, and earth. If these elements are balanced, the seasons run their normal course. When the *ki* of yin meets the *ki* of yang, trees and flowers bloom. *Fusui* practitioners work on the premise that the *ki* of the earth flows in much the same way as the *ki* of the human body, and that the earth has pressure points which can be likened to acupuncture points and accessed in the same way.

It is thought that *fusui* first arrived in Japan from China around the seventh century, close on the heels of other early transplants including Buddhism, Confucianism, and Chinese medicine. The historic city of Nara was originally designed by a geomancer, and Kyoto was also laid out according to one of *fusui's* most auspicious settings, known in Japan as "black turtle, blue dragon, red bird, and white tiger." These are names assigned to geomantic features which, by virtue of their placement and shape, make a setting particularly powerful. However, a *ketsu* location cannot manifest itself until humans create a relationship with the site by placing a building or grave on it. It is the spirit of the place that radiates energy, not the building or grave itself, which acts merely as a means of access.

In Japan today, *fusui* continues to play a role on the island of Okinawa, which has long had close cultural ties with China. Records show that in 1393 a group of Chinese *fusui* experts emigrated to Ryukyu, the former name of Okinawa, and founded the village of Tohei, from which they disseminated *fusui* techniques. Three centuries later, in 1708, the Ryukyu governor Saimon traveled to mainland China, returning with a renewed enthusiasm for *fusui,* and intent on making it the foundation of all city planning. *Fusui* became an official activity within the bureaucracy, remaining so until the Meiji Restoration, after which it was sidelined in much the same way as Chinese medicine in favor of Western ideologies. Even today, however, Okinawans continue to consult geomancers in the planning of homes or graves.

A whole new branch of modern science, geobiology, is based on recent discoveries about the earth and energy lines or fields. In the late 1970s, Dr. Ernst Hartmann, a German physician, hypothesized that a grid of energy lines emanates from the earth's surface and circles the globe. Named the Hartmann grid, these lines were described as being oriented magnetically in north-south and east-west directions at regular intervals, and easily measurable with a simple device called a Lobe antenna. The resulting energy fields were termed "bioelectromagnetic (BEM) fields"; the earth reportedly radiates at least twenty different types of BEM fields, also known as telluric grids. Apparently, Himalayan monks oriented houses and cells for monks in such a way that they were completely contained within BEM fields, evidence, perhaps, that ancient peoples, too, were acutely aware of such energy lines. Researchers today are studying old Chinese *fusui* texts, as well as centuries-old techniques used in Europe, Egypt, Central Asia, and South America. Given emerging knowledge about the body's physical makeup, interplay between human beings and the environment is assuming an even greater significance than before.

Geomancers purported to show that it was possible to divert or neutralize subtle influences which, for better or worse, could affect both the human psyche and thus society as a whole. Claiming that one of the most intriguing aspects of *fusui* is the timing of energy cycles, Mido Ryuji, a Tokyo-based *fusui* practitioner, consults a complicated chart of *fusui* energy timetables and announces that in 1984 Japan entered an energy-down

An alert fox mother restrains her cub at this fox shrine.

cycle that he predicted will last until 2003. Right around the turn of the millennium, the energy flow should begin to improve, until Japan once again enjoys a strong energy surge starting in 2004.

Because both the Earth's magnetic field and the constellations were thought to affect human well-being, *fusui* was critical not only in the siting of all buildings, from the simplest homes to the most elaborate temples and palaces. It also played an important role in the burial of the dead, a cultural practice especially important because of the emphasis placed by East Asian societies on ancestor worship and appeasement of potentially irate spirits. Even *fusui* experts have a hard time explaining how energy can flow from the dead to the living, although Mido theorizes that families share the same cycle or wave of energy. The location of a parent's grave can thus influence a son or daughter. Mido counsels some couples to construct graves while they are still alive, especially in the case of an older man and woman who wish to marry. Since it is unlikely that they will have children, there can be no future energy flow from the union, so Mido selects a site of strong *ki* and has the couple construct a grave that includes their own hair, nails and items of clothing. From this "living grave," the energy can flow out toward the couple while they are living, amplifying their positive vibrations and strengthening their *ki*. For Mido, even the Diet building exhibits *fusui* planning in the way the emperor's seat is located in a special room positioned directly north—a *fusui* power position. On the other hand, he voices concern over the orientation and layout of the Tokyo Metropolitan Government's dazzling high rise complex in Shinjuku, noting that its design and direction make it unable to harness the vital *ki* of its location.

As *fusui* and experiments with *ki* illustrate, Japan's current forays into the mystic frequently draw on reserves of ancient knowledge that have, for one reason or another, been laid aside. Often, however, the advent of the new is actually a return to old awarenesses and strengths, to the archaic depths that may once again yield strategies and solutions for resolving the crises of the modern world. What is now considered supernatural may well be the everyday superpower of the future.

CHAPTER FOUR

Strange but True

Two wooden crosses mark the spot. Facing one another at the top of a shady hill reached by a short series of steps, each cross is surrounded by a white picket fence. Crosses are an unusual sight in Japan, a nation of Shinto and Buddhism where only about one percent of the population is Christian. But even more unusual is the story behind these crosses.

At the foot of the small hill are white boards with inscriptions in both Japanese and English, explaining that this site in a remote Japanese village is the actual grave of

Two wooden crosses mark what are claimed to be the graves of Jesus Christ and his brother, Iskiri. (Photo courtesy of Aomori Prefectural Government)

Jesus Christ. According to the information in English, Christ first came to Japan at the age of twenty-one to study theology. At the age of thirty-one he returned to Judea and tried to preach God's message, but the people, instead of listening, tried to kill him. But it was Christ's younger brother who was crucified, and he died on the cross in his place. Christ himself managed to escape, and, after a long and troublesome voyage, he returned to Japan and this village, where he lived until he died at the age of 106. The grave of Christ is marked by the cross on the right. The cross on the left is the grave of his brother Iskiri, or rather, the resting place of his ears, which Christ brought with him. These facts, says the board, are based on Christ's own testament. Facing the crosses are the carved stone tombs of Christ's Japanese descendants, whose Sawaguchi family crest is taken from the Star of David.

A large Star of David also adorns a tall sign pointing the way to Christ's grave on the main roadway of the village called Shingo, in Aomori Prefecture. This hamlet, located between Gonohe and Lake Towada, was formerly called Heraimura, or Hebrai (Hebrew) Village, a name the locals say came about because of Christ's long stay here. They point to a village culture which is a curious hodgepodge of beliefs and customs with Judeo-Christian links. According to village lore, passed on by those over eighty years old to the next generation, Christ came to Heraimura and decided to stay here quietly without bothering to spread any religious teachings. He did, however, travel all over Japan, visiting many towns, learning about language and lifestyles, and aiding people in various ways. Apparently he was balding, with white hair, a long nose, a red face, and habitually wore a long, crumpled cape. Villagers called him *"Tengu."*

Around the time of Obon, the summertime Buddhist festival honoring the dead, villagers perform a special dance and sing a song, *"Nanyado,"* whose words make no sense at all in Japanese. Upon analyzing them, however, Kawamorita Eiji, a Japanese professor of theology, found the words of the song to be Hebrew; in that language, the song means, "We praise your holy name. We will destroy the aliens [literally, "the hairy people"], and we praise your holy name." The Shinto ceremony here for new babies involves blessing them with the sign of the cross, and when a child takes its first walk outdoors, the parents draw a cross on the infant's forehead for protection. Crosses are also drawn with saliva on the feet when they fall asleep. This ritual is repeated three times for effect.

Obviously, someone did come to Shingo long ago. The fact that villagers believe it was Jesus Christ is an intriguing version of the typical rural tale of "So-and-So slept here." But, then, Aomori is filled with such odd mysteries and myths. Set at the northern tip of Honshu (Japan's main island) and surrounded by sea on three sides, Aomori is the northernmost of the six prefectures that make up the Tohoku region. Geography has nurtured a hardy and tenacious people with a living tradition of fishing and farming. Villages still hug the shoreline, and centuries-old thatched roofs rise over rice fields. It is an expansive prefecture that offers vistas of unspoiled beauty that include virgin beech forests, cypress groves, sculpted cliffs, lakes and rivers, and even a habitat for snow monkeys.

As described in the first chapter, Aomori is home to Mount Osore and the *itako*. It is also a known location of pyramid power, UFO seekers, ancient ties with possible aliens, stone circles, numerous ghost stories, and all manner of other supernatural connections. With a land area of just over nine thousand square kilometers and a population of only 1.5 million, Aomori is one of Japan's least crowded prefectures. Vast, uninhabited stretches may have much to do with the Aomori native's fascination with nature and mystical phenomena. There is something magical in the beautiful but often lonely scenery that brings to mind things beyond the material world.

In 1935, the year the alleged grave of Christ was reportedly discovered, another Aomori phenomenon was stumbled upon by a Japanese painter. This is the stone pyramid on Mount Towari, in the Mayogatai Recreational Forest, near Sannohe. According to a written mythology of Tohoku discovered in Mito, Ibaraki Prefecture, and kept by the Takeuchi family, Japan has seven pyramids, all of which are older than the pyramids of Egypt. The Aomori stone structure is believed to be the fourth pyramid, and as such it is decidedly unimpressive, coming across as an overgrown mound rather than a deliberately planned stone structure. Examination of the pyramid has determined that the stones are set facing in the four directions. One very large stone, now lying on its face and half-buried, is known as the mirror stone. It is thought that this stone once stood upright and that it has symbols carved into it, but it toppled over in the Ansei Earthquake of 1855. The fact that the summit of the pyramid is aligned with the polestar suggests that the edifice may have been some sort of ancient astronomical calendar. The existence of a small shrine also indicates that the pyramid may have been a sacred place for religious rituals, and one British researcher theorizes that it could have been a location for sun worship. Entrance to the pyramid today is through a small, red Shinto gate called a torii, and visitors can clamber over the stones and ponder their ancient relevance.

An equally enticing question is whether Aomori may have been visited by aliens in the distant past. Some people think this may indeed have happened, especially when they look at the clay dolls known as *shakoki dogu*. Near the village of Kizukuri is a small field which a farmer was plowing as usual when he turned up a curious clay figurine resembling an astronaut. Its bulky, ornate costume, with elaborate headgear, has been described as a spacesuit from antiquity. The most intriguing feature, however, is its oversized goggles, similar to those worn by skiers today. In fact, *shakoki* means "goggles"; *dogu* is a clay doll.

Theories about these clay figurines, several of which have been discovered, abound. Some researchers say they were used for funerals, since most were found smashed and buried: the queer face of the *shakoki dogu* could have been a death mask. Others remain convinced that they portray visitors from another world, especially since the dolls are so unlike anything that might have come out of Japan's Jomon era (8,000–200 B.C.E.), a neolithic culture based on hunting, gathering, and fishing, with pit dwellings for homes. Hints about the lifestyle and customs of the Jomon people have been gathered largely from the refuse heaps and shell mounds scattered around their settlements.

Throughout Aomori, as well as in neighboring Akita and Iwate prefectures, the relics found at various archaeological sites underscore this dynamically creative period of Japan's Stone Age. For more than one thousand years, the northeast region now known as Tohoku was evidently a thriving cultural center. Most characteristic of the Jomon era is the intricate *jomon* (literally, "cord-patterned") earthenware, of complex design and exquisite craftsmanship. According to a diary kept by the Kitajima family, who from their base at Nameoka Castle governed south Tsugaru in Aomori during the early seventeenth century, much rare pottery was found in their day. Enthusiastic collectors flourished in the Edo era, and buying and selling of pottery took place even in foreign countries, as awareness of Jomon artwork spread.

But first-class pottery fails to explain adequately the costume of the *shakoki dogu,* which could have been nothing like the everyday simple dress of Jomon people, who hunted with bows and arrows and fished with bone fishhooks and harpoons. Is this fantastic clay doll simply the product of an artist's rich imagination? Or was it created to capture the memory of an alien connection that was celebrated thereafter in careful ritual? Today the 34.5-centimeter-tall statue fortuitously found by the farmer is showcased at the Tokyo National Museum, where it still retains its ancient secret. The field, on the other hand, has become an Aomori tourist attraction marked by a

Do the clay dolls known as *shakoki dogu* recall visitors from outer space? (Photo courtesy of Aomori Prefectural Government)

towering white plaster replica of the figurine, an enormous reminder of the world's many unknowns.

Another mystery turns up at Oyu, a small resort in Akita, between Lake Towada and Hachimantai. In the foothills southeast of the town stands the Oyu Stone Circle, thought to date back some four thousand years, to Japan's prehistoric age. Considered the best example of approximately thirty similar stone circles located throughout Tohoku and also in Hokkaido, the Oyu Stone Circle is actually two large circles, one situated inside the other. Between the perimeters of the inner and outer circles is a sundial, with rocks laid out like spokes radiating from this center. The stones were dragged from some twelve kilometers away, a considerable distance at the time. The Oyu Stone Circle was serendipitously discovered by government surveyors in 1931, and the site has since been designated as a historical relic. As with the *shakoki dogu,* there are numerous theories to explain the circle's existence. More recently, the site was used to fuel military propaganda touting Japan's cultural superiority during World War II. At other stone circles have been found pottery of rare design, such as collections of small-lipped vases. Often, dug under the stone circles, there are oval hollows with diameters of 1.5 meters and depths of seventy centimeters. These may have been used as graves or for special worship. Researchers also believe corpses may have been buried with arms and legs folded into the body with the head facing west. As a graveyard, the circle could have started out small and increased in size. The foundations of Jomon pit houses, partially underground dwellings that were once covered with straw roofs supported by poles, can still be seen at Oyu and other sites throughout Tohoku. Experts so far cannot agree as to whether the bones that have been found are from Japanese, Ainu, or even an older race. Others argue that the Oyu Stone Circle has nothing to do with graves, but is instead a primitive calendar that has astronomical significance only.

Going farther north, to Hokkaido, there is a stone mystery of a different sort. At the coastal town of Otaru is the Temiya Cave. Discovered in 1866 by a stonemason, the cave contains wall carvings that are now thought to belong to the Jomon era. The cave became famous after Enomoto Takeaki, a Japanese politician, stopped over in Otaru in 1878 after a stint of duty in Siberia. Visiting Temiya Cave, he sketched the carving and brought a tracing of it back to Tokyo. A British teacher at what later became part of Tokyo Imperial University traveled to Otaru the following summer and publicized information about the cave in the newsletter of the British Society of Tokyo. Soon, numerous scholars took up the trail, with one report in 1914 concluding that the characters were of Turkish origin, probably carved before Japan's Nara era (646–794), and that the cave was a tomb. In 1918, the scholar Nakanome Akira published a paper stating that the carvings were indeed ancient Turkish, and meant

Researchers are unable to agree about the significance of the Oyu Stone Circle, Japan's answer to Stonehenge. (Photo courtesy of Ozuno City Tourism Office)

"I crossed the sea at the head of my followers and fought and arrived at this cave." He, too, believed the cave to be a tomb, and also that the cave writer had fought in battle with early admiral Abe no Hirabu in 660. Then, in 1947, a local historian and elementary school principal in Otaru, Asaeda Fumihiro, declared that the carvings were actually Chinese characters from around 1000 B.C. According to him, they meant "People came with many ships and built a shrine here. Our king died and was buried here. There was a battle and a religious service with sacrifice." Critics such as Kono Jokichi and Kida Teikichi dismissed all of these opinions, asserting that the carvings were recent, made sometime during the end of the Taisho era (1912–26) or the early Showa era (1926–88). The most vocal critic was the president of Sapporo Hokushin Hospital, Sekiba Fujihiko, who claimed that the head monk of the local shrine at Temiya, a certain Shirano Kaun, had confessed that one of his disciples had admitted carving the figures for fun. This seemed to close the controversy until in 1950 a student at Sapporo South High School found another cave in neighboring Yoichi City, with similar carvings. The next year, the vice-president of Hokkaido University, Natori Takemitsu, began to investigate and discovered more than two hundred such carvings there, in a cave now known as Fugoppe, possibly from an Ainu word. Today the carvings at both Temiya and Fugoppe Caves are considered genuine, perhaps relating to the religious rituals of the multifaceted Jomon period.

The Jomon era is not Tohoku's only enduring cultural legacy. Although in modern times the region has come to be regarded as a backwater, especially by people from big-city Tokyo, Tohoku boasted a "golden age" eight hundred years ago that was based on actual deposits of gold.

Marco Polo's account of Japan as a country of palaces with roofs and floors of gold is thought to have been inspired by rumors of Tohoku gold. A very real and lasting example of such legendary wealth can be seen in the Iwate city of Hiraizumi, headquarters in olden times of the powerful Fujiwara clan. Boasting in its heyday more than one hundred thousand inhabitants, Hiraizumi became widely known for its highly developed Buddhist culture and showy temples. At the Chusonji temple, the Konjikido, the fabulous golden pavilion constructed in 1124 to hold the remains of three Fujiwara lords can still be seen. Although small in size, the building is spectacularly wrought in gold leaf, inlaid mother-of-pearl, and lacquer, and is a convincing testament to Hiraizumi's former splendor. Its beauty has been designated a "National Treasure."

While gold wealth can be conspicuous in the extreme, Tohoku also offers a setting that showcases the most stringent of ascetic practices. Toward the south, in Yamagata Prefecture, is a sacred mountain area known as Dewa Sanzan, a name that refers collectively to the three neighboring peaks of Haguro, Gassan, and Yudono. Dewa Sanzan has long been the religious retreat of a severely ascetic sect, the mountain priests called *yamabushi*. Rituals of the *yamabushi* combine mystic elements drawn from primitive animism and shamanism, as well as Taoism, Buddhism, and Shintoism. They train their bodies to live on these slopes in the depth of snow country by purifying themselves through meditation, fasting, sleeping outdoors, and chanting while standing under icy waterfalls. Also known as *shugenja, yamabushi* were once discredited by the Meiji government, which denounced them as outright phonies, but they and their stringent training have survived to this day.

The most rigorous of practices, however, was undertaken by the "living mummies" of Gassan, who had to remain celibate and give up eating meat and also eventually rice, wheat, and other grains. For a time they subsisted only on mountain vegetables and fruits and nuts, with the quantities of food gradually growing smaller until the amounts dwindled to almost nothing. The body, too, shrank and dried out, and the monk would over time turn into a stringy "living mummy," who, thus transformed, would die in his chosen holy spot. To prepare for dying, the monk usually retreated to a specially constructed chamber constructed below ground. The ceiling of the chamber was so low that one could not even stand upright, and it was connected to the surface by a bamboo pipe which let in air. There, the monk would sit cross-legged, chanting and ringing his prayer bell continuously until he died.

A famous example of a mummy is displayed at the Churenji temple, on Mount Yudono, where it sits inside its own altar. Known as Tetsumonkai, this dehydrated body with grinning skull is clothed in the vestments of a high-ranking monk: orange robe, purple and saffron sash, and a golden hood. For those who come to worship here, it offers proof of someone who succeeded in his goal of becoming a living mummy. But there are many more who failed, and Churenji is said to be haunted by the ghosts of those who could not achieve their spiritual aims.

According to the head monk, Sato Eimei, Churenji is a highly unusual place around which numerous spirits are wandering. He himself has seen a spirit on the roof, another in the cherry tree, and one more in white standing before a tomb, as well as the spirit of a monk unable to complete the mummy training successfully. He has also seen children accompanied by a woman clad in the traditional heavy robes of the Heian aristocracy, and he believes these ghosts call the temple home. One of his strangest experiences was being lifted out of his bath by an unseen force and dropped some distance away into a big, wooden tub. Checking the quality of his morning shave one day, he found that a long beard had immediately grown in. To deal with this supernatural event, he at once ritually purified himself.

Women workers at the temple also report bizarre happenings. A glass door shook so violently that one worker thought it was an earthquake. The head monk, however, said it was the spirit of someone about to die, and sure enough, that evening one of the worker's close

The mummified remains of the monk Tetsumonkai, who succeeded in becoming a "living mummy." (Photo courtesy of the Churenji temple)

acquaintances died unexpectedly. Another temple worker recalls the ringing of the doorbell, followed by the
sound of footsteps in slippers. But when she went to look,
nobody was there.

Ghosts or no, even now ascetics come to Churenji to
undertake a thousand-day period of training, during
which time they eat only gingko nuts and walnuts, the
purpose being to rid the body of excess water in prepara-
tion for becoming a living mummy. And each year, in the
latter part of August, a period of strict training on Mount
Haguro manages to attract believers from throughout
Japan and from varying walks of life. The path of the ascetic, even for those accustomed to the conveniences of
modern living, retains strong appeal.

While grown men and women train at Dewa Sanzan
to become mummified, another Yamagata locale boasts a
fish that may have yearnings to be human. At Tsuruoka
City is the Zenpoji temple. Behind the temple is a garden
and pond in which there lives a fish with an eerily human
face. As it swims toward the edge of the water, its features
appear decidedly unfishlike. There are apocryphal stories all over Japan of fish with human faces, but this is
reportedly the first one whose existence has been conclu-
sively proven. At the center of the pond stands a statue of
a dragon deity, and locals say that it is not surprising that
such a spiritual, mystical place should have a special,
mystical fish.

But it's not only fish in Japan that may have aspira-
tions to be human. In Gifu Prefecture, in central Japan,
there stands a persimmon tree that is believed to grow
human hair. The tree can be found at the Fukugenji temple, in the town of Yoro. Many supernatural happenings
are said to have taken place at this temple, frightening
away even the monks, and today no monk lives there.

Behind the temple, in the cemetery, is a persimmon tree which old-timers such as Yamahata Arakichi swear is haunted. At night, the tree is often enveloped by an eerie blue light, and when the alleged hair growing on a branch of the tree is burned, it smells like human hair. Over the years, the tree has become associated with bad luck and accidents. Several decades ago, for instance, two young villagers decided to remove the hair from the tree. Within a month, one youth developed a fever and died; the other died in an accident. In 1978, a group of hikers visited and picked persimmons from the tree. Returning home, they, too, had a very bad accident.

As the history goes, in 1681 a certain Ishii Mitsunojo's father was killed by Akabori Gengoemon in Osaka. The son, then a twenty-six-year-old samurai, pursued his father's killer to take revenge, but instead was himself murdered by Akabori, who then fled to safety. Almost twenty-nine years later, the third and fourth Ishii sons, Genzo and Hanzo, finally traced Akabori's whereabouts and killed him. Ishii Mitsunojo lost his life when Akabori dragged him by the hair and cut his throat. Ishii's body was buried under the persimmon tree, and people say that his deep sense of revenge shifted to the tree, which absorbed the nutrients from his body and began to grow human hair. At one point, the mature tree fell over, but a new tree sprouted, also bearing hair. Next to the tree is a small stone memorial to Ishii, whose spirit is still believed to haunt the spot where he died. In 1971 a professor at Tokyo Agricultural University examined the hair and declared that it was a really a plant that closely resembles human hair. But locals here remain unconvinced and for safety's sake never come too near the persimmon tree that glows blue in the night.

Human hair is also the focus of a temple, this time in

Hokkaido. The Mannenji temple houses the "Okiku Doll," a thirty-centimeter-high Japanese doll that was the beloved toy of a girl named Okiku. When the temple first received the doll, its hair was cropped. It has since grown to be some twenty-five centimeters long, reaching almost to the doll's knees. Every March 21 has been designated the doll's hair-cleaning day, and although the hair is regularly trimmed, it allegedly grows several millimeters again within a few months.

The tale behind this doll concerns a boy named Suzuki Eikichi, who visited Hokkaido in 1918, probably to see the marine exhibition. On Tanuki-koji, Sapporo's famous shopping street, he bought this doll for his two-year-old sister, Okiku. On January 24 of the next year, however, Okiku died suddenly. The bereaved family placed the doll in the household altar and prayed to it every day in memory of their lost daughter. Over time, they noticed that the doll's hair had started to grow. In 1938 Suzuki and his family moved to Sakhalin, and the doll was offered to the Mannenji temple. People believe that the dead girl's spirit clung to the doll, where it resides today. One examination of the doll supposedly concluded that the hair is truly that of a young child.

Sapporo also draws people eager to snap the ghostly image of a woman with long hair sitting in the Heiwa Waterfall, which cascades prettily in the city's Nishi Ward. When the weather is right, local residents and tourists alike line up with cameras focused on the spot in the river where the woman's image appears. The waterfall has been featured in several television programs focusing on the supernatural, and there was even a cassette recording made of what some say is the voice of a spirit calling for help. One reporter recalls the feeling of being pulled into the river against his will, and Sato Koshun, a monk of the

Nittoji temple, reports that the same thing happened to him more than twenty years ago. Some power he could not fight dragged him down so that he fell into the water.

Hokkaido even claims its own version of "Nessie," the alleged sea monster of Loch Ness, in the north of Scotland. Japan's Lake Kushiro has a mysterious underwater inhabitant called "Kushii," (from "Kussie") and, as with Nessie, sightings have been regularly reported.

Speaking of underwater inhabitants, Tono City, in Iwate Prefecture, has a resident *kappa,* or family of *kappa.* Local tales tell of the *kappa* attempting to drag horses into the water to eat them, and a *kappa* is said to have written out a testament to his actions, a confession which is still kept by one of the area's families. The Tono *kappa* has been discussed by the ethnologist Yanagida Kunio, who chronicled the Tono vicinity's strange tales in his *Tono Monogatari (Tales of Tono).* Another local family has for centuries been given the honorary title of "family of doctors," because they make and use healing recipes taught to them long ago by the *kappa.* One particularly useful medicine is effective for boils or abscesses, and the paste-like concoction was sold all over Japan up until the early Showa era.

Another working alliance between humans and supernatural beings can be found at Oe, in Kyoto Prefecture. This mountain village of six thousand residents adopted the *oni* Shutendoji as a symbol of economic revitalization by launching a regular festival in his honor in 1982. There is now a Japanese *Oni* Exchange Museum, as well as an International *Oni* Association, established in 1994, with about 350 members. Shutendoji, whose name means "saké-drinking boy," was a legendary demon who lived in the mountains and terrorized the Kyoto area by robbing villagers and kidnapping young women. His story is one of the medieval tales known collectively as *otogi-zoshi*.

In the year 987, many people, especially girls of the aristocracy, had gone missing in the Kyoto area, all said to be victims of Shutendoji. So the court astrologer, Abe no Seimei, finally divined the demon's whereabouts on Mount Oe. One of those missing was the son of Fujiwara Michinaga, and this powerful lord informed Emperor Ichijo (986–1010), who ordered four samurai to destroy the demon. They refused out of fear, and the emperor then dispatched Minamoto no Yorimitsu and Fujiwara no Yasumasa to kill Shutendoji. After praying for strength at several Kyoto shrines, the two warriors and their followers set out on November 1, 995. En route, they met an old, white-haired man who advised them to change their costumes to those of *yamabushi,* and to hide their armor in their baggage. Shutendoji apparently liked not only saké, but also mystic seekers. The son of Fujiwara Michinaga was a devout disciple of the Buddhist Tendai sect, and many benevolent demons had gathered to protect him after his capture, confusing Shutendoji, who proved unable to get close enough to kill him.

The warriors then encountered an old woman who claimed to have been kidnapped by the demon more than two hundred years previously. Because her muscles and bones were so hard, the demon had spared her and instead made her his washerwoman. She directed them to Shutendoji's hideout, a grisly scene of rotting corpses, mounds of bones, and assistants preparing human sushi. Pretending to be lost in the mountains, the group begged for overnight shelter. Shutendoji, who appeared as a clever-looking boy, agreed, and spent the night drinking and talking about himself and his exploits. Before coming to Mount Oe, he had lived on Mount Hiei, leaving only because the founder of the Tendai sect also had chosen to live there. Shutendoji had tried to scare off the monk by transforming himself into a huge, menacing camphor tree, but the monk saw through the ruse, and ordered the tree to be cut down. Shutendoji escaped to Mount Oe, where he had been hiding since 849, awaiting his destiny.

At last Shutendoji fell into a drunken slumber, and the warriors prepared their attack. During sleep the demon assumed his true form, a monster with a great red body, the left foot black, the right foot white, a blue left hand, a yellow right hand, and an enormous head with fifteen eyes and five horns. Four samurai held him down as Minamoto and Fujiwara tried to cut off his head, with Shutendoji shouting orders to his helpers to fight. When the head was cut off, it flew in a rage and sank its teeth into the helmet of Minamoto, who used his sword to gouge out two of the demon's furious eyes. When the head dropped, the group carried it back to Kyoto, where it was publicly shown and then placed in the Byodoin temple.

At Oe's Japanese *Oni* Exchange Museum, more than two hundred masks of demons from around the world have been collected, and the library has some four thousand books and documents concerning devils and demons. There are also about fifty demon roof tiles, some dating from the sixth century. Such roof tiles are still used in Japan as good-luck charms to drive off malevolent forces that may mean harm to the house and its inhabitants. To date, the association between Oe and Shutendoji, considered a dicey move when it was first proposed, seems a success. The once-sleepy village now attracts more than two hundred thousand people a year.

Between Kyoto and Tokyo, on the old Tokkaido highway, is a famous stone known as the "Nightly Weeping

Rock." A pregnant woman in the Edo era was traveling to meet her husband when she was attacked and murdered by a robber. Her blood spilled on a large rock, which embodied her spirit and each night began to weep. A detailed rendering of this poignant legend was made by the print artist, Utagawa Kuniyoshi (1797–1861), who portrayed the bereaved husband holding the newborn baby in his arms as the ghost of his wife relates her sorrowful tale. Legend has it that Kannon, the Goddess of Mercy, had somehow rescued the child and reared it on a diet of sweets. In one version of the story, the ghost then aided the unhappy widower in avenging her untimely death.

Another talking rock is said to be found at the Monju Senji temple, in the town of Kunisaki, in Oita Prefecture, Kyushu. A human voice, heard by several persons undergoing Zen training here, issues from the stone statue, but so far nobody has been able to catch the meaning. A stone tomb at the Daisenji temple, in Iwate Prefecture's Morioka City, on the other hand, sounds like metal when it is tapped. This granite grave marks the burial place of Okan, the daughter of a samurai who served the Nanbu clan and area. Even now, Nanbu ironware is famed for its skilled craftsmanship. After Okan married, she rejected the approaches of a would-be lover, who then killed her in anger. Her husband then became a monk, and Okan was revered as a symbol of the virtuous, loyal wife.

CHAPTER FIVE

Modern-Day Hauntings

Old Edo has long since burgeoned into the megalopolis that is modern Tokyo, a sprawling mass of glass, steel, ferroconcrete, and tarmac crammed into two thousand square kilometers. Visitors impressed by this almost ceaseless kaleidoscope of glare and action seldom encounter what lies just beneath the frenetic East meets West facade. Nevertheless, under the dazzle of commerce and industry beats a primitive heart still attuned to the world of shadows. A legacy of East Asian supernatural beliefs remains. Today's Tokyo may be a global economic center, but ghosts and other such phenomena are very much a part of everyday life, found even in the most contemporary of places.

A convincing example is the business district of Otemachi, now known internationally as an important hub of Japan's banking and trading activities. Just beside the hundred-meter-tall building that houses the headquarters of the Mitsui Trading Company stands a monument so unobtrusive that most people walk by without giving it a second glance. For the businessmen who work in the vicinity, however, this monument is a solemn reminder that unhappy spirits have the power to disturb. It is said to mark the burial place of the head of Taira no Masakado, a disgruntled samurai who lived during the Heian period, which takes its name from Heiankyo, the old name for Kyoto. Toward the end of the eighth century, Japan's capital was moved from Nara to Kyoto, which remained the center of government until the late twelfth century. In 939, planning to set up an independent state, Taira no Masakado named an alternative capital in Sashima, in what is now Chiba Prefecture, and declared himself the "New Emperor." His rebellion, however, was short-lived; the following year, he was killed by Taira no Sadamori and Fujiwara no Hidesato.

As the legend goes, he died from an arrow wound, after which his body was beheaded and the head displayed in Kyoto as a warning for other would-be rebels. But three months later the head was unchanged. In fact, people said it looked the same as when he was alive, except that now the eyes were especially fierce and the mouth grimacing even more horribly in death. One night, the head, enveloped in a glowing light, is believed to have taken off and flown toward Taira no Masakado's home in what is now Ibaraki Prefecture. On the way, it was shot down by an arrow fired by a monk at Atsuta Shrine, which today houses one of Japan's three sacred treasures. The head dropped to Shibazaki Village, where the villagers picked it up and buried it beneath a mound in Kanda Myojin Shrine. Some ten years later the mound began to glow and shake violently. The ghost of a haggard-looking samurai appeared regularly until special prayers offered by the terrified villagers seemed to put the spirit to rest.

Later during the Edo era, Kanda Myojin was moved to a new site, but the tombs were left behind. In the Meiji era, the Finance Ministry constructed their building nearby, but it burned down in the Great Kanto Earthquake in

The head of Taira no Masakado is said to rest in this grave in Otemachi.

1923. In rebuilding, the ministry destroyed the tombs and erected a temporary structure on the site. This proved to be an unfortunate decision. Reportedly fourteen officials of the ministry, including the finance minister himself, died within a short period. Many other workers became ill or were injured. Reconstruction was abruptly halted while a purification ritual was held. The ritual continued to be held every following year, with less and less enthusiasm as time passed, until something else happened. On June 20, 1940, on a day of heavy rain and thunder, the Finance Ministry caught fire. People remembered it was exactly one thousand years since Taira no Masakado's death, and the finance minister ordered and announced a special remembrance ceremony.

Reports of various unexplained phenomena around the site continued for the next twenty years. In 1945, U.S. occupation forces cleared the site to create a parking area. Again there was sudden death and serious injury. This parking area was removed in 1961 so that new construction could begin, and just in case, each corner was purified with ritual salt, and the tomb once more dedicated to Taira no Masakado. These gestures seem to have been insufficient. Once construction was complete, workers in the rooms facing the tomb routinely fell ill. Many white-collar workers from nearby offices grew quite nervous, especially with reports that people who tried to take pictures around there often saw a face with disheveled hair in the camera lens. The construction company, extra cautious, had already begun the practice of praying at the tomb on the first and fifteenth day of each month. Then, the practice broadened. In fact, neighboring companies jointly formed the Taira no Masakado Memorial Committee and the bank adjacent to the tomb went so far as to send an employee from the General Affairs department to pray on the first day of every month. Sanwa Bank likewise ordered an employee to visit and pray at the tomb once a month. The bank president is also said to have donated the tomb's donation box for the mere reason that his building cast the tomb into shadow.

Today, Otemachi businessmen remain guarded about this tomb in their midst. Supposedly nobody wants to work with his or her back toward the tomb, nor does anyone like to directly face it. Even the mass media takes precautions. Whenever mention is made of Taira no Masakado or his tomb on television programs, for example, the film crew visits the site to pray. Japan may be an economic juggernaut, but Japanese leaders, at least in this business center, seem determined to ensure that one unhappy ghost will not disturb international wheeling and dealing. He may have failed to make himself emperor, but more than one thousand years after his death Taira no Masakado is still wielding his influence.

What's more, this influence may be extending far beyond Tokyo. In the small town of Tazawako, in Akita Prefecture, stands the tomb of Taira no Masakado's daughter, Princess Takiyasha. The Tohoku area became a refuge for members of the Taira clan seeking safety, and Princess Takiyasha was buried here in this sheltered spot. Now, visitors to the tomb say that after sleeping for more than one thousand years, she is beginning to appear again, with her likeness materializing on one of the small, wooden memorial tablets, or *kifuda,* at the grave.

In December 1992, for example, someone named Sato Chuji videotaped what he and many other visitors believe is an image of a beautiful woman, with palms pointed upward in prayer and wearing a white kimono. On either side of the figure stand what look like two retainers, and people seem convinced that the image is that of

Princess Takiyasha, and that it has considerable drawing power. According to Nakamura Meiko, the nun who serves as the head monk of the faraway Ryugenji temple, in Koide, Niigata Prefecture, a figure stood by her pillow one night, asking Nakamura to come to the grave in Akita, and to bring her monk's robes. Nakamura obeyed, and has reported that standing at the grave, she felt compelled to kneel down and say, "I am here now." As she did so, the image appeared, a woman with long hair and red

Fireballs were sighted near the Sunshine 60 high-rise in Ikebukuro.

lips, in a white kimono. The nun asked the age of the image, and a voice replied, "I am seventeen years old." More surprised than frightened, people are now speculating as to why Princess Takiyasha should have awakened after more than ten centuries of silence in her tomb.

Another breaker of silence is the ghostly weeping in the Diet building, the seat of Japan's central government. After World War II, the eighth floor of the Diet was used by U.S. occupation forces as a dance floor and school for office workers. According to the story, one woman, disappointed in her love for a man at the dance club, jumped from a window, breaking her neck. Shortly after, that the weeping could be heard. The eighth floor was then closed off under the pretext that it was for the purpose of "defense of public morals." Until 1977, there was a red aircraft alert on the ninth floor, and security personnel used to check this every month. After the taller Kasumigaseki Building was constructed, however, the light was removed. Today, few people venture up to the eighth or ninth floors, so there is almost no one to listen for the sad weeping for unrequited love.

Another Tokyo building with supernatural links is the 240-meter-high Sunshine Building, completed in 1978, in Ikebukuro. In August 1979, around the anniversary of the end of World War II, fireballs reportedly appeared above the Sunshine Building's open area. The fireballs were sighted by a third-year high school student who looked up around 10 P.M. and saw three fireballs, which he thought at first were UFOs. Two additional fireballs then appeared, hovering in the sky. After about five minutes, all five fireballs disappeared. In Japan, fireballs are thought to symbolize the dead, and before the practice of cremation became so widespread, they were often sighted, especially in or around cemeteries.

The Sunshine Building and the six-thousand-square-meter Higashi Ikebukuro Central Park stand on the site of the former prison where seven Japanese war criminals, including Tojo Hideki, were executed on December 23, 1948. After the executions, a memorial was built. In 1964 it was designated a historical ruin, and two years later the Tokyo Metropolitan Government decided to convert it into a park. The actual prison facilities were moved to a new location at Kosuge, in Saitama Prefecture, in 1971.

For several years, however, construction was delayed because no company was willing to accept the work, which was considered potentially unlucky. Work finally started in earnest in 1978, but during the construction there were many troubling incidents. Three workers were hurt while taking down a thick concrete wall. Another worker heard a ghostly, groaning voice. Yet another who had to work at a tomb ran away from the construction site and was eventually hospitalized in a mental institution. One worker took a picture of the old prison wall before it was destroyed, and the photo contained an extra image, of a Buddha statue wearing a military cap. Construction of the park was completed in 1980 and a stone monument erected, wishing eternal peace. So far the spirits seem appeased, although fireballs are still seen from time to time.

Until the mid 1970's the Nichigeki, near Yurakucho, was a popular entertainment hall. Able to seat more than three thousand, it featured a variety of shows such as chorus girls dancing the can-can. In 1970, a dancer known as Suzuki (neither name in this anecdote is real), was cast as the lead. She had joined the show along with 250 other women, but only six from the original group remained. The day before the first scheduled performance, Suzuki died in a traffic accident. "The curtain will rise shortly," were her dying words. Her close friend, Kimura, completely cleared out Suzuki's dressing table, but when she returned later she was shocked to find a photograph of Suzuki there. The next day Kimura, arriving early at the Nichigeki, encountered another dancer, dressed and ready to perform. It was Suzuki, her clothing covered in blood, making sure she was there when the curtain rose.

Iwanami Hall, in Kanda, is also known for the many strange mishaps that occurred while *Tokaido Yotsuya Kaidan* (related in detail in Chapter VII) was being staged there in 1976. First, in the November before the play's premiere, the playwright Uchiai Kiyohiko was hospitalized with what began with stomach pains and toothaches. A subsequent fall in the hospital resulted in a head wound that required stitching. In January, one of the main actors was leaving home for a meeting about the play when he fell down and was brought to hospital in an ambulance. The following month, the actress playing Oiwa felt something amiss when she was eating in a sushi restaurant with four other members of the cast and the waiter brought six cups of tea. When six sets of sushi were also brought, she asked why, and was told that the sixth set was for the other woman sitting there. Incident followed incident, with actors and actresses either falling or being affected by sudden and unusual swellings on their hands. One actor was riding his bicycle at night when a woman emerged suddenly from the shadows, causing him to fall. When he got up she was gone. Badly frightened, he quit the show. Just before the play's opening, another actor contracted measles, and the day before the opening, the mother of the actor playing Oiwa-san's husband died suddenly. Then a young scene shifter had his hands mysteriously trampled on, breaking his bones. Of course, the entire cast and related personnel knew they would have to keep praying at and visiting the shrine of Oiwa-san in

Yotsuya. It was a year when the spirit of Oiwa-san was particularly restless.

Close to Yotsuya was a Shinjuku supper club, Stardust, run by Shibata Toku. A well-known singer, she opened the club in 1979, and of course invited many entertainers. The door to the club was quite heavy, and creaked loudly on its hinges when opened. Often the door creaked although nobody was there. At other times, people saw a shadow, but heard no sound. Shibata is said to have declared that she frequently felt that someone was watching while she worked. She saw shadows, too. These phenomena only happened on rainy nights, around 1 A.M. At such times the heater refused to work. Gradually, the shadow at the front door materialized to the point that one night a customer asked about another customer sitting there; the club owner could see no one else.

On May 14, 1979, it had been raining very hard and was quite cold. There was only one customer at the club when, just after 1 A.M., the front door creaked and banged, and a short-haired, middle-aged man wearing a yellow cardigan entered. Upon being greeted by a hostess, he vanished. Later, there was again running water in the empty men's toilet. The next day, just past midnight, a customer pointed out that a new customer had just entered, a woman with long hair and wearing a black dress. When the owner went to look, there was no one. One hostess, recalling the previous night's events, became thoroughly frightened. Everyone began to sing folk songs to gather courage. But it had been too much to tolerate. In the morning, the owner called a moving company and shifted everything out of the club, which was subsequently destroyed.

In the Hongo area, now home of Tokyo University, there used to be, in the Edo era, a vegetable shop named after the owner's daughter, Oshichi. In December 1682 there was a big fire in Edo, and Oshichi escaped to a temple, where she spent the night with its caretaker. Returning home, she began to reason that if there were another fire she could run off to the temple again. She then set a number of fires until she was found out and arrested. The following year, at age sixteen, she was burned to death at the stake for arson, a punishment deemed appropriate for what was seen as a heinous crime. Fires were so common in old Tokyo that they were rather proudly referred to as the "flowers of Edo," but cramped wooden housing conditions meant that such flowers could be deadly. Her tomb was placed in the Enjoji temple, at Hakusan, but during the air raids of World War II, this temple burned down. Later, a bookbinding company was built nearby and workers thought they heard a door creaking and the sound of geta. Even NHK came to record the sound, but failed to do so, and the subsequent release of the program resulted in several letters from viewers saying that they, too, had heard the sound of geta. A popular NHK quiz show, "Twenty Doors," would ask questions of participants, and immediately the correct answers would be written on strips of paper and revealed to the audience. At a show staged at the Matsuya department store in Asakusa, one of the answers written was "The Ghost of Oshichi." When the paper was displayed, the audience fussed aloud, so that the NHK show host went to investigate. The message mentioning Oshichi had mysteriously disappeared, leaving only a blank strip of paper to be held up to the audience.

Mystery also surrounded the Kawasaki City Gyokusen branch of the Nakahara Fire Station, about fifteen minutes on foot from Hirama Station. On October 29, 1980, fifty-two-year-old Okuma Isamu was sleeping as usual in the lower bunk on a second floor area. He was awakened around 2 A.M. by someone pressing against the right side of his chest. At almost the same moment, someone entered the bed from where his left foot was. This person gave Okuma a distinctly unpleasant feeling. At the time, Okuma did not really know what was happening, and later joked with a coworker about the man and woman who had entered his bed. Two days later, the same thing happened again, this time around 4 A.M. He tried asking his colleague to turn on the light, but found he could not speak or move. He then saw a man and a woman who looked at him for a while before disappearing into the wall. The man was in his mid-thirties, with a longish face. His naked upper body was muscular, but he had no legs. The woman, of average height and build, wore kimono, and had a round, expressionless face, her head held to one side. She, too, had no legs. Okuma felt that the man, who gave a severe impression, belonged to the early Showa period.

In 1982, Okuma wrote about his experiences in the newsletter *Fire Kawasaki.* An overwhelming response from colleagues showed that many others had had similar experiences. Out of thirty-two firemen at that time, for example, one-third had seen the ghosts. The next year, on January 29, a twenty-five-year-old foreman, Akiyama Mikio, saw the torso of a ghost, and when Fire Chief Nakajima reported it to the head fire office, they in turn recounted the background history.

The fire station and its twenty-meter-high watchtower were built in 1959, right at the edge of the cemetery attached to the Hottaji temple. The hauntings are said to have started almost immediately thereafter. A middle-aged woman wearing a white kimono was seen climbing the tower, and the sound of ascending footsteps could be heard at midnight. When the ground was cleared for the tower's construction, many human bones were dug up. At that time, all the firemen prayed at Hottaji and held a special service for the dead before each of the tombs. The tower was destroyed in 1980, but a new building was erected in its stead. Ghosts again appeared in the spot where the watchtower once stood, now a sleeping area for firemen. New construction had resulted in the collection of two cement bags' worth full of human bones which people believed belonged to unknown persons, or the families of tombs interred in Hottaji's tombs. Old-timers, however, said that there were wetlands as well as rice farms here before, and that the bones could have shifted a long way in the soft ground.

Wealth had come to this town originally because it could supply gravel and small pebbles, or *jari-jari*. People had come from afar just to work in the pebble industry, which was so important that even the babies here are said to have cried *jari-jari*. The bones may have belonged to migrant workers. Once again, the fire station held a service, and in 1982 raised a memorial stone over a square hole dug four meters deep and filled with pebbles. All money for the stone had been donated, and it was decided to offer incense, flowers, and food on the first and fifteenth day of each month. The ghosts were laid to rest.

A peace of sorts is also believed to have come to the Tokyo horse racing tracks near Fuchu. The tracks were moved from Meguro to Fuchu in 1933, and right from the start people said that the third curve was demonic. Between 1965 and 1974 especially, numerous serious accidents took place there. In 1966, three horses collided on the third curve, and crashed into the barrier. In 1971, Suinoza, ridden by the jockey Marume, attacked another horse, badly injuring Marume, who had to retire. During the Emperor's Cup race in 1972 the first and second favorites to win suddenly lost their energy at the third curve and could not run. The same thing happened to top horses at exactly the same spot in 1973 and 1974.

People in the horse racing business can be very superstitious anyway, and the incidents convinced many that the third curve was haunted or manifested some supernatural activity that was spooking the horses. For one thing, nearby were thirty-two old tombs belonging to the Ida family. The Idas served the prestigious Hojo family based at Odawara, and when the Hojos came under siege the Idas escaped to Fuchu. The Tokyo Metropolitan Government purchased the racetrack land through various real estate agents and requested the landowners to move the tombs. This was strongly refused. In the end, the city opted to preserve the tombs as a type of historic ruin. Horse trainers swore that horses would always stop abruptly at the zelkova trees near the tombs and then bolt in fright. This was credited to animal intelligence and the fact that horses have a keen "sixth sense" which enables them to perceive psychic phenomena.

One by one, the big zelkova trees were cut down, until only the largest was left standing. It had three thick branching limbs, and it was planned to cut these one after the other, and finally the massive tree trunk itself. When the gardener who sawed off the first limb died suddenly of unknown causes, no second gardener would come forward. After several years, the second limb was removed. That gardener also died immediately afterward. At last the zelkova tree toppled over by itself in a typhoon in 1978.

Long-time residents here also say that the area was once a marsh containing many white snakes, which are considered sacred messengers of the gods. In the years following World War II, however, when food in Tokyo was extremely scarce, some people overcame their awe and ate even the white snakes. Those foolhardy folk are said to have died after their meal. To appease what might well be supernatural forces at the Fuchu racetrack, a statue of the horse god, Bato Kannon, was erected in the 1970's. Things seem to have quieted down since.

Slightly farther west is the long-established town of Hachioji, now a commuter suburb for Tokyo company workers. The name Hachioji means eight princes, and one explanation of its origin is that Amaterasu and Susanoo together created five gods and three goddesses. Another story says that Susanoo had eight children, five boys and three girls. Whatever its etymological roots, Hachioji is acknowledged to be a gateway to limbo, and there are several easily accessible routes to the nether world. Among these is Shiroyama Rindo, a narrow, woodland track at the ruins of Hachioji Castle. A half-rotten wood marker points the way along a shady, usually deserted path, where the only sounds are a burbling stream and a rock occasionally falling.

The former site of Hachioji Castle is itself another spot where the living can encounter the dead. Erected around 1570 by Hojo Ujiteru in Japan's civil strife period, Hachioji Castle in its heyday extended over a vast 154-hectare area. Hojo was a powerful feudal lord who placed his foothold in Odawara (currently Odawara City, in Kanagawa Prefecture), and ruled the surrounding region, choosing as his supporting god the deity called Hachioji Gongen. Over time the surrounding village that grew up around the castle assumed the name Hachioji. In 1590 Hachioji Castle was invaded by an army under the command of Toyotomi Hideyoshi, who later unified Japan as shogun. The castle was seized on June 23, and on that day many women leapt from the castle walls to their deaths, rather than fall into the hands of the enemy. There was so much death and slaughter that blood was said to have run like a river into the waterfall, even turning the rocks red. The ruins of Hachioji Castle were left untouched for four hundred years, until they were designated a histori- cally valuable site in 1951. Today it is designated a nation- al relic, and excavation studies have been undertaken here since 1977. But much grudge and resentment are believed to have lingered on. On June 23 of each year, the surface of the water is said to turn red, a reminder of a fateful day of loss.

Overlooking Hachioji City, about two kilometers from Hachioji Station, is the 213-meter-high hill known as Otsukayama. Set in a clearing among the gnarled, old trees are the ruins of a small temple, Doryodo. The tem- ple was shifted from Asakusa to this site in March 1873, by Watanabe Taijun, who enlisted the financial support of the area's prosperous silk merchants. At one time, a "silk road" used to run from Hachioji to Yokohama, and along it was transported silk gathered from growers through- out the Kanto plain. Around the turn of the century Doryodo, although small, was a thriving temple backed by the active silk trade.

A ghost began to be seen here from 1965, and, even now, people say they can hear a woman's weeping among the trees. This unhappy spirit is said to belong to Asai Toshi, who died horribly on September 10, 1963, at the age of eighty-two years. The old woman was found mur- dered inside the main temple building. Her throat was cut, and she had been stabbed through the heart. Her killer had then thrown a cushion over the dead body and made off with about three million yen that Asai Toshi was known to have been hoarding.

An illegitimate child, Asai Toshi was twenty-eight years old when she entered the Doryodo temple to assume the duties of caretaker. In this role she also told fortunes for the villagers. She also bore several children out of wedlock. Her first son was born in 1918, but he died shortly after birth. Three years later she had a daughter, who also died as a baby. On September 1, 1923, the same day as the Great Kanto Earthquake, Toshi gave birth to a second

The ruins of the once-impressive Hachioji Castle are now said to be haunted by unhappy spirits.

daughter whom rumor had it was fathered by the temple's monk. The first person to find Toshi's dead body was this daughter, Michie, who was forty years old at the time, and she placed her mother's tomb in the tiny cemetery just behind the temple.

Surrounded by a simple bamboo fence, the cemetery is reached by five deep stone steps. To the right as one enters is a headstone for dogs and cats, and inside are eleven memorial stones, including one raised by Asai Toshi in memory of the temple's founder, who died at the age of eighty-four on October 8, 1916. A marble, two-tiered stone topped by a globe of the same material marks the grave of Asai Toshi. Beside it is the waiting grave of her still living daughter, Michie. Her name is carved on the stone in red to indicate that she is still alive. When she dies, the engraving will be colored black. There is also a grave for the girl and boy who died shortly after birth, as well as a large stone for the entire Asai family. But peace seems to be difficult for the restless spirit of Asai Toshi, whose body in the world of the living met such a violent death. In 1983 the abandoned Doryodo temple was finally destroyed, and in 1990 Hachioji City designated it and the surrounding hillside as Otsukayama Park.

To possibly encounter yet another supernatural experience, head toward Mount Takao along the route of the old Koshu Kaido highway, now Route 20, one of the five major routes used during the Edo era. Lined with traditional Japanese-style houses, many of which are formerly inns for travelers going to and from Tokyo, this winding road seems to belong to another age. At Kobotoke was a crucial checkpoint set up by the Tokugawa government. From 1623, four guards were posted here, and people could travel to and fro between the hours of 6 A.M. and 6 P.M., provided they could show their authorized passes. Travel throughout Japan was severely restricted, and anyone caught circumventing the checkpoint was crucified, a situation which lasted until 1869.

At the entrance to what used to be Route 20, at Kobotoke Toge, there is a tunnel haunted by a ghost. Here, at night, a woman holding her baby appears suddenly, causing startled drivers to have accidents. One man saw the woman smile and disappear. Another person recalls in fright that the woman approached the car, looked closely in his face, and intoned, "wrong man." People say the woman was hit by a car and left lying. Others believe she is searching for the man who abandoned her and her baby. Whatever the reason, she now materializes without warning and vanishes when the car skids or crashes.

Cries from the past can often be heard in Yamanashi Prefecture, which more recently gained notoriety as the

Only ruins remain of the Doryodo temple, where Asai Toshi was murdered.

main base of the AUM cult. At a place called Oiran Buchi, literally meaning "prostitute gorge," people can sometimes hear the screams and cries of women. In the surrounding hilly area gold has been found since the Heian period, and during the Edo era there was a gold mine here, with brothels for the miners. The gold belonged to the wealthy Takeda family, but after the Takeda fortunes were ruined, it was decided to kill the fifty-five prostitutes working here to stop the rumor spreading about the gold available. The killers constructed a wide, wooden platform, suspended above the steep gorge, and invited the prostitutes to drink and dance there. At the height of the revelry, the ropes holding the platform were slashed, and the women plunged, screaming, to their deaths. Further downstream the villagers at Tabayama were able to fish the bodies out of the water, and they built a memorial to the victims there. Today, visitors, especially men, are cautioned to be wary of standing too close to the edge of Oiran Buchi, where the screams of angry spirits still echo.

Entrances to limbo can be found at a number of tunnels in and around Tokyo. The Sendagaya Tunnel, between Harajuku and Meiji Jingu, runs beneath the cemetery of the Senjuiin temple, and is a site of hauntings. Bad *ki* is said to flow from the cemetery and accumulate in the tunnel and drivers passing through have been startled by the face of a woman or a child in the windscreen. Another story tells of the woman who hails a cab, only to vanish when the taxi door opens. The Shirogane Tunnel is feared among taxi drivers as a place where Death incarnate, or Shinigami, awaits. Agonized faces have appeared on the tunnel's pillars, and the number seen seems to be increasing. Along Route 134, between Kamakura and Zushi, is a spot considered to be one of the most mysterious in the entire Kanto plain, a place where energy is absorbed. Even locals avoid it. At a nearby tunnel, a human face will suddenly appear on the car's rear window, or hand prints unexpectedly may be seen on the windscreen.

Modern hauntings take place not only in tunnels, but on bridges from which people have jumped to their death, as well as hotels, inns, and apartment buildings. Screams of the dying are said to have terrified security guards at the gutted ruins of the Hotel New Japan in Nagata-cho. Due to the owner's carelessness, the hotel was destroyed by fire in 1982, killing thirty-three guests. The blackened structure was an eyesore, as well as a spot to stay clear of, and no buyer could be found for the property until July 1995. Nobody wanted to inherit a hotel haunted by spirits of human beings tragically burned to death.

At Inawashiro, in Fukushima Prefecture, there is a so-called "ghost pension," an enormous derelict inn where several people say they have encountered various spirits of the dead. One Japanese psychic, Watanabe Shizue, in 1995 accompanied a television crew investigating the haunting. Claiming to have seen the ghost of a man in his sixties standing in the garden, and that of a white-haired woman in kimono at a second-floor window, she believes these are the spirits of a married couple. But the history of the pension is unclear, and nobody seems to know why it was abandoned and left to rot.

In neighboring Miyagi Prefecture is the Daigyoji temple, on Mount Tomiyama, in the town of Matsushima. It has been a center of worship for some 1,200 years, and many spirits are said to be wandering here; the temple bell rings by itself even when there is no wind or anyone around. The bell is most likely to ring between one and two in the morning. Also heard at night is the sound of water being taken up and poured from the famous well,

Suigetsu, in the temple grounds. Again, there is nobody there, although the head monk, Inatomi Koun, tells the story of how one night he went to investigate the sound and saw, standing at the well, a young woman who then disappeared. In addition, he recalls that one evening, around eight o'clock, he watched as a fireball about thirty centimeters in diameter approached from the outer gate, and headed toward him. The fireball veered upward and flew into the main temple building.

Beginning in 1985, there was a problem of haunting at a large apartment building constructed approximately eight minutes or so away by foot from Kanazawa Hakkei Station. The mansion was reportedly built on the east ruins of the Jokoji temple, where there were more than forty tombs dating back to the Middle Ages. Numerous strange happenings have been reported in the area. A ghost wearing armor appeared in a certain room at night. A woman in another spot was visited at night by the dark figure of a large man beside her bed. For some reason she was unafraid, because she felt he was trying to ask her something, but when she tried to use her voice, she could not. Another time, the temple's deputy head monk, Kurata Shoin, was walking with his four-year-old nephew on the hill behind the ruins, when the little boy suddenly became deathly afraid and grabbed his uncle. A man living in the neighborhood was walking his dog, when, she, too, became terrified near the ruins and ran away to safety. The monk felt that children and perhaps also animals, have special psychic power which enables them to sense the presence of spirits. Intriguingly enough, there was considerable controversy over the building's construction, especially after several hundred human bones were dug up from the ruins. A number of people strongly in favor of the construction reportedly died suddenly of unknown causes, or met with serious accidents. But construction of the mansion was eventually completed in 1988, and a prayer service held, asking the spirits not to haunt the residents. So far they have honored this request.

Then there is the haunted prefectural museum in the Naka district of Yokohama. During the Sixties, several museum exhibition workers heard a groaning voice and saw a woman in kimono wandering at night on the third floor. In 1977 one worker heard a woman's very loud screams, and later that year footsteps were heard. Previously, the site had housed a local bank, and on the day of the Great Kanto Earthquake, some two hundred residents escaped to shelter in the bank's basement, along with 140 bank employees. Although the basement walls were thick, the people inside supposedly heard the terrible screams of people outside begging to be let in. At about half past four in the afternoon, all fell quiet, and the basement door was opened. Several hundred corpses lay strewn about.

During 1928–29 there was financial panic in Japan, with many people and businesses going bankrupt as the silk exporting industry collapsed. Local citizens reportedly asked the bank (Shokin Bank at that time) to bail them out, but the bank refused. As a result many families committed suicide. The building later became the Yokohama branch of the Bank of Tokyo, and then was remodeled as the museum. These sundry spirits are said to haunt the museum today.

Some say the Fukoku Seimei Building, in Uchisaiwai-cho, is haunted by an unfortunate office worker who threw herself out of a high window to her death. Her body supposedly fell into the bushes, so that it was not discovered until several weeks later. Office ladies who now ride in the elevator have reported feeling a female presence standing behind or beside them. Often the elevator buttons light up by themselves, as if some unseen person had pushed the floor indicator.

Perhaps to reflect the more harried pace of modern society, ghost stories in Japan have grown shorter, as if people no longer have the time for long, elaborate tales. But the point is that the storytelling continues. Brushes with the paranormal remain a favorite media topic. Moreover, interest and research into supernatural phenomena other than hauntings is greater than ever. Mysticism and science seem to be merging in a sincere attempt to seek solutions to life's unanswered speculations.

Throughout the rich tapestry of Japan's history, the supernatural has been an enduring thread that is simply being reworked to meet the emerging needs of twentieth-century civilization. New worlds and possibilities are unfolding at a sometimes dizzying pace. The hidden life of the mind has assumed increasing importance. Awareness and appreciation of human potential is growing.

Like so many people seeking answers, Japanese are rediscovering that there is much more to humankind than meets the seeing eye. With the approach of the twenty-first century being loudly touted, it will be fascinating to watch what develops from now, given current research and discoveries. As the history of the supernatural in Japan shows, human beings are an intrinsic part of both the mystic and the mysterious. The essential unknown is woven into the daily fabric of our lives. For this reason alone, Japan's search for the supernatural has continuing relevance for us all.

CHAPTER SIX

Scenes of Ghosts and Demons

As night deepens, a group of people gathers to play a game of daring. One hundred candles are lit and set behind blue paper. By the flickering light, each group member, one after the other, narrates a ghostly tale. As each story is recounted, another candle is extinguished. Bit by bit, the room grows darker and still darker. At last, the final candle is put out. Now there is only a silent blackness. Huddled together, the storytellers shiver. It is the moment to await what the darkness might bring . . .

Like people all over the world, Japanese love ghost

stories, and the scarier the better. In creating just the right atmosphere blue is chosen because it is thought to be the color of *hito dama,* or the spirit as it leaves a newly dead body. Blue lights sometimes hover above graves, or are seen gliding out of houses. Use of the number one hundred, simply signifying numerous, dates back to one of the oldest beliefs about the supernatural in Japan, the *hyakki yako,* or "night parade of one hundred demons." Popular since the Heian period, the belief in *hyakki yako* is based on the premise that night is the time when goblins and ghosts appear, ruling the hours of darkness before disappearing again at dawn. Out of this belief came the basis for the game *hyaku monogatari,* or "one hundred eerie tales," with its form of storytelling well established by the middle of the seventeenth century.

These days in Japan, telling ghost stories is still popular as a summertime activity. The sweltering month of August is now characterized by crushed ice and haunting tales. This is, after all, the time of *Obon,* when dead relations are invited home for remembrance and feasting before they are sent back to the spirit world in paper lantern boats or astride miniature steeds fashioned out of eggplant. At shrines and local parks everywhere, even in central Tokyo, men, women, and children wearing *yukata,* or cotton summer kimono, dance to the drumbeat of *Obon* rhythms around raised platforms lit by lanterns. There have been many accounts of ghostly encounters taking place during these circular dances for the ancestors. It is an ideal season to dwell on the strange and the supernatural.

In Japanese thought, when a person dies, the spirit leaves this life, bound for an eternal world. Before reaching this destination, however, the spirit must spend some time in an in-between plane of existence, a limbo of vague uncertainties. It is while detained in this state that a spirit can become a restless or unhappy ghost set on haunting or otherwise disrupting those with whom it still feels a strong connection. Thus, powerful emotions of hatred, revenge, sorrow, or jealousy can create a ghost, drawing a spirit back into this world to wreak its havoc. Such ghosts continue to haunt the earth until someone or something releases them back to limbo to resume their journey to eternity.

During Japan's Edo era many such ghosts were female. Although ghosts and ghost stories had been part of Japanese culture for centuries, it was in the Edo era that strong interest in the supernatural was revived. This may have been because this long era in Japanese history was one of social upheaval in which creation of class structures imposed severe restrictions on common people. Perhaps the reemergence of a panoply of supernatural phenomena, including ghosts, demons, and changeling animals reflected the unrest within society. Or perhaps it was simply an age that craved the thrilling and the mysterious. Especially exciting was the idea of a wrathful female ghost returning to exact vengeance for former mistreatment.

Edo era artists typically rendered the female ghost as a fragile form with long, flowing hair and beckoning hands. Dressed in pale or white clothing, the body below the waist tapered into nothingness. Japanese people today still imagine ghosts as lacking feet, and having arms that are bent upward at the elbow, with hands hanging pathetically down from the wrists. In tales from this period, the extent of suffering a person experienced while alive directly influenced the actions of the spirit after death: a wronged woman could return as a particularly nasty ghost. A range of ghostly female emotions is showcased in the *Ugetsu Monogatari (Tales of Moonlight and Rain)*, compiled by the writer Ueda Akinari (1734–1809).

Nor was the ghostly world populated only by females. Male ghosts, too, had their place, and indeed, were among the most popular characters in kabuki theater, which allowed for superb dramatic effects when a ghost came on stage. Kabuki convention dictated that the ghost's face be pale blue, with eyebrows brushed in silver and lips smudged blue or black. As befitted a wandering spirit, the hair was disheveled, hanging loose around the shoulders. The popular art of ukiyo-e, another Edo-era creation, also depicted ghostly beings, with one of the best-known being Utagawa's print of the ghost of Sakura Sogoro, the hero of the kabuki play, *Sakura Giminden (Legend of Sakura, a Man of Justice)*. Often grisly in their details, kabuki ghost plays like this nonetheless were meant to convey the sense that evil inevitably gets its comeuppance. There was eventual balm for even the most grotesque suffering and bloody violence, and justice would finally prevail.

In addition to ghosts there are *yokai,* or *obake* (monsters). *Yokai* stories are found everywhere in Japan, with different regions having their own versions of the same story line. *Yokai* do not arise spontaneously, but are shapes reflected in the mirror of the deepest psyche. They thus show all the bad deeds of which human beings are capable of doing. They are the dark side of our nature, manifestations of our worst imaginings and fears. Forever lurking in the deepest recesses of our minds, *yokai* are always seeking the chance to surface. Extraordinary shapeshifters, they can change their form into anything they want, anytime. The childhood bogeyman, the monster of the dark, the dreadful shape that looms in the corner, all these are ages-old reminders of our murky past and the part of ourselves we would prefer not to face. At the appropriate time and place, *yokai* appear once more, terrifying in intensity and malevolent will. Alongside a lonely rice field. In the forest at night. Out of the whirling snow.

In addition to Shutendoji and Tamamo no Mae, major *yokai* in Japanese folklore include Zegaebo, the Chinese *tengu* who came to Japan in 966 to frighten Buddhist monks, but failed miserably. There is also Sutoku Joko, born in 1119, the first son of the unlucky Emperor Toba who was victimized by Tamamo. Deeply embittered by his politically blighted life, he died cursing, biting his tongue so that he could write his last hateful oath in blood. After death he fulfilled his vow by becoming the great king of ghosts.

Momiji was a female demon, while Tsukumoshin tells the tale of monsters born out of the resentment of discarded tools. When they reach the age of one hundred years, tools can become spirits, so most people throw out tools long before then. To give themselves a greater chance of survival, a group of disgruntled tools planned to use the celebration of *setsubun,* the first day of spring on the lunar calendar and a time of renewal, as their chance to enter the heart of creation, or emptiness (*mu* in Buddhist doctrine). Here, where the eternal flow of yin and yang creates new matter, they believed that they, too, would receive spirits. They thus became monstrous *yokai,* killing humans and animals and drinking their blood. Another *yokai* was Princess Hashi, whose thirst for revenge transformed her into a living demon.

Demons, or *oni,* of course, are almost always troublemakers in the human world. A female demon, the *shiko-me,* is first mentioned in the *Kojiki.* Today, female demon masks are still common, and many a Japanese household has a mask representing a jealous, vengeful woman with

CHAPTER SIX

two horns sprouting from her head. Demon quellers, with their power to devour goblins and their evil ilk, are associated with the festival known as Boys' Day, held every year on May 5.

But insight into Japanese ghosts and demons is best gained by looking at the stories themselves. The following selection collected from around Japan and translated anew here offers an intriguing glimpse into regional folk tales and supernatural beliefs.

* * *

Shadow Woman

This tale comes from the Tohoku region, which comprises the six prefectures of Akita, Aomori, Fukushima, Iwate, Miyagi, and Yamagata.

In the clear Akita moonlight, a woman's shadow falls in the doorway of a house at the far end of the village. The woman raps at the door, awakening Sakube. Stumbling out of his sleep, he opens the door. An icy wind blows in. Shrouded in the night is the black shape of a woman cradling a small bundle, a baby only days old. Instinctively, Sakube draws back. Who are these midnight visitors and why are they here? The woman replies that she is lost and unable to give milk, and needs some rest. Sakube relents and welcomes her in, taking the baby from her arms. Immediately the woman disappears into the cold, night wind. With a scream, Sakube sees that the baby has grown fangs and a black, hairy covering all over its body. In a panic he throws it down, and it, too, disappears into the cold night wind. From that moment on, whenever there is a chill wind at night, the same woman arrives outside Sakube's house. Driven mad, Sakube abandons his home

and nobody sees or hears of him again. Shadow Woman
has been too much for him.

* * *

Muddy Rice Field

> *This tale comes from western Japan. In this nation of rice
> culture, people everywhere believe that when a rice field is
> left uncared for, a spirit or monster moves in. Or, there
> might be some supernatural entity keeping people away.*

In Bizen, in Okayama Prefecture, there was a rice field
that people said was the really the home of a *yokai*. Out of
fear, nobody in the village went near it. It was also said
that the water in the rice paddy was bottomless, and cer-
tainly many animals had already drowned there. Yet, every year, this field produced an excellent harvest, although
nobody was ever seen tending it. One day, a traveling monk
from faraway heard the ringing of a temple bell near the
field and went to look. At once the *yokai* loomed out of
the paddy and grabbed the monk. As he disappeared into
the depths of the rice field, the flowers of the rice changed
from white to blood red.

For much of Japan's history the more rural parts of
the Tohoku area have been very poor. The practice of
infanticide, or baby weeding, was common. Babies who
were discarded and left to die are said to have become
zashiki warashi, or "parlor children," destined to haunt
houses throughout the region.

Some three hundred years ago in an Iwate village
there lived a wealthy man called Masaimon. Everybody
liked him because he was also very kind. So it was a great
surprise when an itinerant monk arrived at his house one
night and murmured that Masaimon would soon be com-

pletely ruined. After the monk left, Masaimon began to
brood about the traveler's words. The more he worried,
the sicker he became, until, feverish and hallucinating,
he came close to death. As he was lying down one night,
he could hear the sound of footsteps running lightly above.
Abruptly the footsteps stopped. A small voice just over his
head whispered, "Are you dead? Are you dead?" Then
water began to drip down on his face from the ceiling.
"Limbo is very cold," whispered the voice again. Suddenly a small child appeared, wet from head to toe. Terrified,
Masaimon lost consciousness. When he came to he heard
the shoji screen sliding open and then closing. There was
a sound of brushing, then the shoji surrounding the room
started to shake violently. A child's laughter pealed out
and there again was a small boy standing over him. "Are
you dead? Are you dead?" whispered the child. This was
too much for Masaimon, who died of fright. Soon afterward the fortunes of his house, as predicted, rapidly de-
clined. His family was ruined.

* * *

The Eyes

*And then there is the story about a temple haunted by myriad
eyes, or* mokumokuren.

Nobody could recall when the Mokurenji temple had last
had a head monk. The temple had long been abandoned
and the only inhabitant was thought to be a fox or a *tanuki,* which was sometimes glimpsed during the day. Villagers used to dare one another about going there after dark.
Young people used to tease each other that the man brave
enough to remain in the temple until dawn would be given
a night with the most beautiful girl in the village. But still,

no one went there. After one autumn festival, however, a group of young men became quite drunk and made a bet with a traveling peddler, Yoshimaru. He took them up on their dare, and fortifying himself with saké, entered the temple. As he sat drinking, he heard strange sounds, but he continued until he fell asleep in a drunken stupor. In the middle of the night, he was awakened by a loud noise, and, looking around, he saw eyes peering in everywhere through the many holes in the old shoji. The young men waiting nearby outside could hear him screaming, "The eyes, the eyes!" Then, the shoji began to fall down, with Yoshimaru still crying aloud. After that, there was silence. When dawn broke, some young men crept into the temple. They found nothing but a bloody rag and what may have been Yoshimaru's eyes. No one ever talked about the incident again.

In Japan today, children still play a game called *niramekko,* where two people stare into one another's eyes. Each makes a strange face, daring the other to laugh. The one who laughs first loses. It is said that whoever plays *niramekko* with *mokumokuren* is sure to lose his or her eyes.

* * *

Old Mountain Woman

Among the monsters in Japan are the female mountain ogres, who like nothing better than to eat human beings. Varying versions of this story are found throughout Japan, especially to the west and south.

A hard-working family lived near a mountain. One day the mother had to leave the house and, as usual, she cautioned her three sons not to open the door for anyone, no matter what reason. Everyone knew that an awful ogre inhabited the deep forest high up the slope, and several people had disappeared. After she had gone there was a knock at the door. "Who is it?" asked the oldest son.

"I am your next door neighbor, and I need help. Please open the door."

"Your voice is too strange," replied the boy. "I won't open the door."

A short time later, there was another knock at the door. "Who is it?" asked the youngest son.

A voice sweetened with honey answered, "I am a good friend of your mother's. She has a message for you."

"Show your hand at the crack," ordered the boy. A grizzled, hairy hand appeared. "I see by your hand that you are really the ogre. I won't open the door," said the boy.

Shortly afterward there was another knock at the door. "Who is it?" asked the middle son.

"I am your mother, and I'm so tired. Let me in," said a feeble voice.

"Show your hand at the crack," the boy replied. A hand newly shaved and powdered white appeared. The middle son hesitated, but at last opened the door. At once the ogre jumped in and devoured him. The other two sons managed to run out of the house, the ogre in pursuit. By the river grew a tree so tall that it was said to reach heaven. The two boys reached the trunk and began climbing as fast as they could. Further and further they climbed, as the ogre, heavy and panting, tried to follow. When the ogre had reached high enough, the boys took some stones they were carrying and dropped them on the ogre, who lost her balance and plunged from the tree to her death. Her monster blood spilled out, deeply soaking the earth. And that, say the Japanese, is why the roots of the soba plant, the source of beloved buckwheat noodles, were forever turned to red. In yet another version of story the older son additionally becomes the moon, the younger son a star.

* * *

Ancient Tree

In rural Japan, some people believe that once a tree becomes more than one thousand years old, it changes into a spirit which can be well-intentioned or quite malevolent. In some places they say that when a woodcutter dies in the forest, his spirit turns into a yokai.

The woodcutter Musabi no Gen goes up the mountain to cut wood. As he tries to hew down a large, old tree, however, he hears a voice murmuring, "Be careful, I'm going to fall down, get away." Startled, he looks around, but seeing nothing unusual, continues his cutting. The voice repeats the words and this time the woodcutter cries aloud, "Who's there?" The only reply is the sound of a tree falling. He jumps back in alarm, but no tree actually falls. Determined to persevere, the woodcutter keeps on until it grows dark. As night falls, the tree begins to change in the most horrifying way. Eyes and mouth appear on a writhing trunk. From the gnarled roots rises a blue light, the spirit of the tree. Stubborn Musabi no Gen is enveloped by the tree and is seen no more.

* * *

Simple Dwelling

But if the realm of yokai *can be terrifying, the world of human spirits can show such virtues as loyalty and love stronger than death. Indeed, these are common themes in the* Ugetsu Monogatari, *from which the following story comes.*

A merchant named Katsuhiro has to visit Kyoto to sell silk. His wife Miyagi, a woman of great beauty and strong character, is very worried about this new business ven-

Has this old tree awakened into a dinosaur-like monster?

ture. She also knows that it will be difficult to manage
financially without her husband, but she nevertheless
helps him prepare for his long journey. On the eve of his
departure the couple talk fondly, with Miyagi sad about
life's uncertainty but promising that she will be waiting
for his return, day and night. Katsuhiro consoles his wife
by promising that he will be back by autumn, when the
leaf of the arrowroot will be rippling in the wind.

That summer, however, fighting breaks out, and Katsuhiro is caught in the turmoil, unable to go home. When
autumn comes with not even so much as the slightest
rumor of her husband, Miyagi grows depressed at his faith-
lessness and unreliability. Writing her grief in a poem she
asks the rooster to tell her husband that autumn has
passed.

The political situation throughout the country
worsens. Miyagi considers fleeing to safety but recalls her
promise. Then a new toll gate is built, requiring travel
permits, but Katsuhiro has no papers. Again he is
trapped. Resigned to his situation, he remains in Kyoto.
Miyagi, in the meantime, loses all her money when she is
robbed by a servant who runs away. Her beauty also attracts many suitors, all of whom she rejects. With the
country at war and no place truly safe, Katsuhiro imag-
ines his wife to be dead. Seven long years pass, and finally
things settle down enough for Katsuhiro to return home.
Arriving back, he is relieved to find his old house standing intact, although the rest of village is desolate. And
there, beautiful and strong as when he had last seen her,
is his beloved wife Miyagi. It is a joyful reunion, each shar-
ing the sorrow of separation and hardships endured
before lying down to sleep. When Katsuhiro awakens
next morning he finds that Miyagi has gone. Soon a
wandering beggar informs him that Miyagi died years

before. Katushiro has slept with her ghost, a spirit that kept her promise to be waiting for his return.

* * *

Chrysanthemum Promise

Fierce loyalty is also featured in this story.

A monk named Sanmon came to know Soyenmon, a scholar of military tactics. When Soyenmon fell ill it was Sanmon who took care of him, so much so that the two men pledged to become blood brothers. Soyenmon had to return home, but promised to meet Sanmon again later that year, on September 9. When the day arrived, however, it was not Soyenmon himself, but his ghost who came. While home, he had been arrested and detained by his cousin, who had plotted against him. Knowing that he would thus be unable to keep his promise to Sanmon, Soyenmon had committed suicide so that his spirit could come instead. A distraught Sanmon then traveled to Soyenmon's hometown and killed the cousin, avenging Soyenmon's death. After that, Sanmon himself disappeared.

* * *

Blue Mask

Then there is this tale of strange determination.

When Kaian, known to be a virtuous Zen Buddhist monk, visited a mountain village in present-day Tochigi Prefecture, the villagers feared he was a demon. When he asked why, the people told him about another monk, living on the mountain, who became so depressed about a young boy's death that he ate the corpse. Villagers therefore mistook Kaian for another flesh-eating monster disguised as a monk. So Kaian went up to the mountain temple to visit this monk. The monk attacked Kaian, planning to devour him. Failing in the attempt, however, he asked Kaian to help him spiritually. Before he left, however, Kaian gave the monk a blue mask and a special sutra, instructing the monk to chant it. The following winter Kaian visited the mountain temple again. The monk was still there, grown incredibly thin and still sitting and chanting the sutra. Kaian lifted his staff and gave the monk a sharp whack. Immediately the monk disappeared. All that remained was a crumbling pile of bones and a blue mask.

* * *

Princess Hashi

In this tale, also known as *Hashihime,* the wife of Yamadazaemon Kunitoki had bit by bit driven herself crazy over the fact that her husband kept a concubine. Although she many times pleaded with her husband to give up the woman, he ignored her pleas, so she decided to exact revenge. Near her house was a shrine where people visited at the hour of the ox (between 1 and 3 A.M. in the traditional Japanese clock) to ask favors of the gods. For seven consecutive days, the same time every day, she prayed to become a living demon.

On the seventh night, she stayed at the shrine, and it was the shrine priest who dreamed that the god agreed to grant the woman's earnest request. But first she had to don a red kimono, paint her hair red and divide it like horns, and wear a three-pronged iron crown, in which fires should be lit. After that she had to sit in the Ujigawa river for twenty-one days. She would then become a living demon.

Her husband, meantime, had a series of horrible nightmares which he asked the court astrologer, Abe no Seimei, to explain. The latter warned him that he could lose his life as a result of a woman's revenge, so the man confessed to having made his wife madly jealous by keeping a concubine. The astrologer gave precise instructions for the man's protection, so that when the living demon, his former wife, broke into his bedroom one night and stood by his pillow, she was unable to exert any power over him.

Unable to take revenge as she had wished, she stalked the streets of Kyoto each night, terrorizing the citizenry. Upon meeting a man, she would change into a beautiful woman he could not resist. When she met a woman, she became a handsome man. Either way she killed the hapless victim she had cleverly bewitched. Eventually nobody dared go out at night, so the emperor ordered Minamoto no Raiko to find her and destroy her. Raiko dispatched two disciples who cornered her one night after a long chase. Surrendering, the living demon vowed to cease her evil actions, asking them to mourn for her after death, and promising to become the palace protector. She then jumped into the Ujigawa and drowned. When the emperor heard this story he held an elaborate funeral, where one hundred monks chanted sutras. Soon after, the demon appeared in a dream to the emperor's servant, requesting that a shrine beside the Ujigawa be built in her honor. The emperor complied, and erecting the shrine, he renamed the unhappy woman Princess Hashi of the Ujigawa.

CHAPTER SEVEN

Edo-Era Tales

By the late eighteenth and into the early nineteenth century, Edo joined the ranks of the world's great cities, with its population exceeding one million. By comparison, the population of Europe's largest city, London, had not yet reached one million.

Vigorous and dynamic, Edo was a center of popular culture that gave birth to many things now considered quintessentially Japanese, among them kabuki, sushi, and woodblock prints. It was in this culturally bustling metropolis that ghost stories enjoyed a new heyday.

The following tale of supernatural love, which borrows elements from China, is once again based on an actual incident that took place during the Edo era. Encho, the famous storyteller, told his own version to enthralled audiences during Japan's Meiji period. The poignant tale is here reworked anew.

* * *

The Peony Lantern

THE MAD FATHER

Some two hundred years ago, in Tokyo's Ushigome district, there lived a samurai called Iijima Heizaemon. After the sudden death of his wife he was left alone with his daughter, Otsuyu, but he soon married again, this time to his former servant, Okuni. Just when Otsuyu reached marriageable age and was ready to begin a life of her own, however, Okuni fell in love with the servant Genjiro, and the two plotted Heizaemon's death by poisoning. The amount of poison they put into his food was not enough to kill Heizaemon, who survived their attack, but with his mind unhinged. Okuni and Genjiro, meanwhile, their murder plot discovered, escaped together.

Otsuyu was deeply disturbed by this unexpected turn, but realized that there was nobody else to take care of her father. She begged him to move to a quieter place where she hoped his mind could rest and eventually recover. Heizaemon agreed, and the two retired to a house in Yanagishima Yokogawa. After the move, Heizaemon passed the time tending the garden and trying to calm his still furious heart. Occasionally, however, he suddenly remembered what had happened to him at the hands of

Okuni and Genjiro. At such times he became completely deranged, and would rage through the house or garden, brandishing his sword and swearing to kill Okuni. Sometimes he even tried to kill Otsuyu, mistaking his long-suffering daughter for his faithless second wife. But each time, Otsuyu controlled her father's mad outburst by talking softly and asking him to recall who she was. Heizaemon would wave his sword wildly about for awhile longer but then would abruptly fall into a brooding silence. This also discouraged Otsuyu, who would again coax her father, gently saying, "Please, father become the person you once were. Become the father I used to know and loved so well." Then she would take her koto, at which she was especially skilled, and play to console the troubled man.

DREAM OR REALITY?

Near the quiet retreat where Heizaemon and Otsuyu lived was a large, wide moat. One day a young samurai, Hagiwara Shinzaburo, who lived in Nezu, came fishing there with his friend, Dr. Shijo. They planned to fish, and hired a small boat for that purpose. As they sat on the water Shinzaburo heard the sound of a koto coming from the house at the far edge of the moat. What a lovely sound, thought Shinzaburo dreamily, losing himself in the plaintive melody. Before he knew it he had left the boat and was standing at the back entrance to the house. The door opened and a servant, Yone, signaled Shinzaburo to come inside. She led him to a room where Otsuyu, the koto player, sat waiting.

With their first glance Shinzaburo and Otsuyu took to each other, and, abandoning any pretense at shyness, began to talk in detail about themselves. "I am Hagiwara

Shinzaburo from Nezu," announced the young samurai. "Both my mother and father are dead and I have been alone in the world, but from now on I hope you will keep a close relationship with me." Otsuyu then explained her own family history, saying that she, too, was glad to have found someone like Shinzaburo. The two talked on like this for what must have been hours. During a pause in their conversation, Otsuyu drew out a small incense burner delicately etched with a design of autumn grass. "I received this from my mother just before she died," said Otsuyu. "Now I would like you to keep it as a token of our deep and lasting friendship."

At the very moment she handed the gift to Shinzaburo, Heizaemon leapt into the room, his sword unsheathed. In an unfamiliar, cracked voice he shouted, "At last the evil man has been found out." Otsuyu, terrified, jumped up to protect Shinzaburo, throwing her body against him. But Heizaemon's sword was swift. Down it flashed, slicing into Otsuyu's body and felling her dead. A shaken Shinzaburo fled into the garden, followed by the still-raving Heizaemon. Unable to find his way out, Shinzaburo was finally cornered. Heizaemon's eyes glittered as he approached with a terrible glee. "This serves you right, Okuni, my wife, and Genjiro, my servant. Now you will learn your lesson." Once more, the sword flashed, killing Shinzaburo at one stroke. Then, Heizaemon turned the blade on himself and committed seppuku.

Shinzaburo screamed as in a nightmare and opened his eyes to find himself awake and alive. Pinching himself he looked around and saw that he was still in the boat. Obviously it had all been a bad dream. His first thought was to tell Dr. Shijo, who sat quietly fishing, but then he heard the sound of a koto coming from the house at the far edge of the moat. And there was something else. Reaching into his kimono, he drew out a small incense burner delicately etched with autumn grass—the very incense burner he had accepted with so much gratitude from Otsuyu in his dream. Now he was unsure about what had really taken place. Seeing the young man's puzzled frown, Dr. Shijo asked what was the matter. But Shinzaburo simply asked whose house it was at the far edge of the moat, from which he could hear the sound of a koto. Dr. Shijo looked up. "Oh that is the Iijima family's house, but I don't hear any koto. You must be imagining it." Shinzaburo looked suspiciously at his friend, but concluded that he was telling the truth. He decided to let the matter drop, and said nothing about his strange dream.

THE SOUND OF GETA

Thoroughly mystified, Shinzaburo returned to Nezu with the incense burner safe inside his kimono. Shortly afterward, an old family friend named Yusai, who had been a trusted advisor to Shinzaburo's father, dropped by to see him. Noting that Shinzaburo seemed depressed, Yusai tried to cheer him up. "I don't know what's bothering you, but surely it can't be that bad. Why don't you try to forget whatever it is and not let it get you down. If you don't dwell on it, the matter will probably clear up by itself in no time." And off he went, leaving behind a listless Shinzaburo who had said not a word about the day's baffling events.

Night fell, and the house and surrounding neighborhood became totally quiet. Everyone was asleep but Shinzaburo, who sat wide awake trying to interpret his dream. At the hour of midnight he suddenly heard the sound of geta, *ka-ran-ko-ron*, faint at first, but coming nearer and nearer until the footsteps stopped right at his front door. A voice cried out, "Shinzaburo, sir, this is Yone. I have brought my young mistress to see you. Please open the door."

"Otsuyu!" cried Shinzaburo, overjoyed in spite of himself and without considering it strange that the two women from his dream should be visiting him at midnight. He opened the door as if he had been expecting this all along. And, sure enough, there stood Otsuyu with her servant Yone, who was carrying a paper lantern with a peony design. Shinzaburo also noticed that Otsuyu was wearing a kimono dyed with the same design of autumn grass that graced the incense burner she had given him. "Come in," said Shinzaburo. From out of the night the two glided into the room, a slight wind stirring as they moved. Shinzaburo saw nothing amiss, either in their style of walking or their faces, which were a little too pale. He was only glad, so glad, to see Otsuyu again. Although he had not yet come up with a rational explanation for his dream and the fact of the incense burner, Shinzaburo willingly abandoned his mental struggle. He sat down with Otsuyu, and the two immediately resumed their intimate talk.

When the first rooster crowed, Yone started and cried out in a frightened voice, "Young mistress, come away right now. Let's finish this night and leave before others find us." The two women glided out the door, a slight wind stirring behind them. Long after they had gone Shinzaburo could still hear the sound of geta, *ka-ran-ko-ron,* echoing in his ears.

THE MONK'S DREADFUL MESSAGE

The next morning, Shinzaburo awoke very late. Finding his energy level low, he did not feel like doing much of anything. Indeed, all he could think about was the coming night and how he longed for darkness to fall so that he could see Otsuyu again. He sat around all day, waiting. Eventually night fell, and midnight came. Again, the sound of geta approached, just like the night before. And there again stood Otsuyu with her servant Yone, carrying the paper lantern. "Come in, come in!" exclaimed Shinzaburo, his vigor returning. And once more he invited Otsuyu into the room, where the two talked ceaselessly until the first rooster crowed.

This continued night after night. Soon, the townspeople began to talk, whispering among themselves that young Hagiwara was spending his nights with a ghost. A rumor arose that outlined against the shoji screen of his room, one could see Shinzaburo's shadow sitting through the night. Worse, facing him sat the shadow of what looked like a skeleton and the two shapes moved as if they were talking. "Dangerous, dangerous," whispered the neighbors, chills running up their spines. But no one dared do anything about the frightening situation.

At last the rumor reached Yusai who, concerned as always, hurried to pay Shinzaburo a visit. He found the young man unperturbed, if a little tired. "What's this I hear about your talking with a ghost?" demanded Yusai, anxiously. "I've been told of your ghostly visitor each night, but it can't be true. Tell me what's really going on."

Shinzaburo remained unruffled. "Visited by a ghost? Of course not. And to prove it, here is the incense burner she gave me when we first met." Yusai saw the small incense burner delicately etched with a design of autumn grass. Then Shinzaburo explained the story from the beginning, telling of his fishing trip with Dr. Shijo and the house by the moat where the koto played, and the subsequent midnight visits.

When Yusai heard Shinzaburo's story, he became extremely agitated and went to see Dr. Shijo to confirm the story of the fishing trip. "Yes, it's perfectly true that we went fishing in that moat," said Dr. Shijo. "But I'm curious why you are asking this now, because the trip was about eight years ago."

"Eight years ago? Not recently?" queried Yusai.

"No, it was around eight years ago. Around the same time we went fishing, I happened to hear the story about the Iijima family that lived in the house at the far edge of the moat. The mad master Heizaemon had just killed his daughter Otsuyu, along with her servant Yone. He then committed suicide and died. The details of this sad story stayed quite vivid in my mind."

Confused, Yusai asked Dr. Shijo to accompany him to the moat where the latter had gone fishing with Shinzaburo around eight years previously. They found Iijima Heizaemon's house in ruins, the once-tended garden overgrown with grass. "It does seem that the family was completely ruined some time ago," mused Yusai. "I don't understand at all, but it is a bad sign."

He then consulted the monk at the Shinbanzuiin temple, where the tomb of the Iijima family was placed. Yusai related all he knew to the monk, who listened carefully, his expression gradually growing more and more concerned.

"If all this is true, then it is indeed terrible," said the monk. "It shows that Otsuyu and Yone are not happy in their graves, and that their spirits are wandering. Now that you tell me this, I realize that the peony lantern at the tomb of Iijima has remained fresh and new without even a single tear for the last eight years. Never once have I seen it torn or damaged in any way, and it is only a paper lantern. I always thought it strange, but now I know what has befallen Shinzaburo."

The monk looked long and hard at Yusai. "I am very sorry to have to tell you this. But Shinzaburo has only a few more days to live."

Horrified, Yusai clutched the monk's robe. "Is there nothing you can do to stop this ghost from haunting Shinzaburo? Nothing at all?"

At first, the monk shook his head. But then he muttered, "It might be possible, there may be a way." He instructed Yusai to take strips of paper on which the monk would write special protective sutras, and place them over every door, window, and other opening of Shinzaburo's house. He also told Yusai to order Shinzaburo to begin chanting at night, and to continue chanting no matter what might happen.

"If my instructions are precisely followed," cautioned the monk, "then the ghost will be unable to enter the house, and we might have a chance of exorcising this demon that is haunting Shinzaburo. I myself will also chant for as long as necessary."

Yusai took the strips and covered all openings at Shinzaburo's house. He commanded Shinzaburo to begin his chanting and not to stop for any reason. Shinzaburo did as he was ordered. In his heart, however, he refused to believe that his beautiful Otsuyu, so lively and so dear, might be a ghost.

THE RUINED PEONY LANTERN

Out of respect for Yusai, Shinzaburo began chanting when night fell. At midnight, as usual, the sound of geta, *ka-ran-ko-ron,* approached and halted just outside his door, now covered with protective sutras. Unable to enter, Otsuyu cried out, "Shinzaburo, please let me in as you always do and let's talk together again."

Although Shinzaburo longed to see her, he refused to open the door, but concentrated and continued chanting, despite Otsuyu's many pleas throughout the night. Finally, the first rooster crowed. The sound of geta withdrew from the house and faded into the distance. The next night, and the night after that, and the next, the same thing happened. Otsuyu and Yone would approach and beg to be let in. Each time, they would leave when the first rooster crowed. For seven nights, Shinzaburo kept up his chanting. At Shinbanzuiin, the monk, too, was chanting, praying that the sutras would soon take effect.

On the eighth night, the sound of geta again neared, and the voice of Otsuyu called out piteously, "Shinzaburo, please open the door. If I could only see you once more, my deepest hope would be realized. I have nothing to live for in this desolate world. Please let me in, Shinzaburo, please."

Although his heart felt as if it were being torn open, Shinzaburo steeled his will against Otsuyu and ignored her mournful begging. For seven more nights, he continued chanting, stepping up his pitch so that he would not have to listen to Otsuyu's wailing at the door. After fourteen days and nights, the sutras did not seem to be having much effect on the ghosts, who continued to arrive at midnight arrived and beg to be let in. But still Shinzaburo chanted.

The twentieth night came. As usual the two women arrived and Otsuyu pleaded, her voice as rending as a koto strain, "Shinzaburo, you never let me see you any more. This makes me so sad. All I am asking is that you let me see you just one more time."

Shinzaburo could hear Otsuyu sobbing. But he rang the bell and clutched his prayer beads, chanting louder than ever. At the first rooster's crow, Otsuyu and Yone disappeared. When he could no longer hear the sound of the geta, Shinzaburo fell heavily against the altar where he had been chanting and wept. "Otsuyu, I, too, want to see you, more than you can ever know. But I cannot, I must not, do it. Please understand this and forgive me. Accept that it is all over between us."

The twenty-first night arrived. Clasping the incense burner inside his kimono, Shinzaburo began chanting. At midnight, the sound of geta approached, *ka-ran-ko-ron.* Otsuyu's voice, now weak and low, called out, "Shinzaburo, tonight is the twenty-first night. This will be the last night that I will come to see you because after tonight I can never come again. This is goodbye."

When he heard her words, Shinzaburo felt a deep sadness wash over him. "Otsuyu, is tonight really your last night to visit me?"

"Yes, Shinzaburo, it must be so. Although I have tried my best, over and over, I am not strong enough to overcome the power of the sutras and your chanting. It means that I can never see you again. Now all is finished. This is the end for me."

Shinzaburo felt a miserable mixture of shock and pity. "If that is so, I know that if I never see you again I, too, will no longer have the will to live. Oh, Otsuyu, I recognize what a terrible thing I have tried to do to you by banishing you."

Then Shinzaburo strugggled to stand up, his body weakened by twenty-one nights of continuous chanting. Mustering his last reserves of strength, he staggered to tear down the sutras and let Otsuyu in. As soon as he opened the door, Otsuyu, waiting for precisely this moment, flew to Shinzaburo and flung herself upon him. At that moment, in the far distance, the first rooster crowed.

Also at exactly that moment, the prayer beads broke in the hands of the monk still chanting for Shinzaburo at Shinbanzuiin. The beads scattered over the floor. Immediately the monk stopped chanting. "So..." he murmured, bowing his head, "So Shinzaburo was still too young. He could not be helped."

The monk understood. He put out the candles at the altar and slowly left the prayer room, his task finished.

Next morning, Yusai went to Shinzaburo's house and was shocked to find every door and window flung wide open. Rushing inside, he called out for Shinzaburo, but stopped and screamed, paralyzed with fright. There on the floor, the incense burner with the design of autumn grass in hand, lay Shinzaburo, dead. With his hair matted, and with a long, unkempt beard, he looked like an old, sick man, emaciated and sucked dry. Yet, when Yusai looked closer, he thought he could see a trace of a smile around Shinzaburo's lips.

Yusai immediately went to Shinbanzuiin to inform the monk, who had done his best to help. Before Yusai could speak, however, the monk said sadly, "Yusai, you have seen the true nature of human beings." And he began to pray.

Then, together, Yusai and the monk walked to the Iijima family tomb. There they found the peony lantern which for the last eight years or so had been kept so new and fresh. It now lay as if knocked over by a strong wind, torn into tatters.

* * *

Tokaido Yotsuya Ghost Story

Some say she walks the streets of Tokyo, a forlorn figure in white, her long hair hiding her face. As she approaches, she suddenly reveals her horribly scarred features, a face twisted by death agonies. When people scream and run in terror, she disappears, laughing.

So goes the story of Oiwa, perhaps the most famous ghost in Tokyo. Her tragedy is the main tale in a mix of separate incidents pulled together for dramatic effect in Tsuruya Nanboku IV's well-known kabuki play, *Tokaido Yotsuya Kaidan (Tokaido Yotsuya Ghost Story)*, more popularly known simply as *Yotsuya Kaidan*. The play incorporates a true account of two murders committed by two servants, each of whom had killed his master.

During the Edo era, murder of one's master was considered on a par with patricide. For such a crime, punishment could be gruesome. The criminal's head might be slowly severed from the body with a bamboo saw—an excruciating death. Alternatively, the criminal might be sent to a workhouse, more akin to a chamber of horrors, where every day was a living hell.

In Nanboku's version of the Oiwa story, a darkened stage is the setting for murder. Iyemon has just killed the father of his young, beautiful bride Oiwa, simply because the victim knew about foul deeds committed earlier by Iyemon. Iyemon is a *ronin,* or masterless samurai, who is now obliged to earn a living as an oilpaper umbrella maker to support Oiwa and their new baby. This affront to his dignity festers into a hatred of Oiwa, which makes it easy for him to succumb to the temptation offered by the granddaughter of a wealthy neighbor. The girl herself is crazy about Iyemon and wants to marry him.

But first there is the problem of Oiwa. The girl's grandfather persuades Iyemon to give the delicate Oiwa what he claims to be a health tonic. Iyemon knows what this really means—that the tonic is, in reality, a virulent poison—but his desire and greed hold sway. One night, he puts the "medicine" into Oiwa's food. Before she dies in agony, Oiwa is shown her face in a mirror. The poison has dreadfully disfigured the right side of her lovely face. Her ensuing rage and resentment are the violent emotions which will fuel her vengeance as a ghost.

Iyemon's wickedness continues. Aware that his servant knows of his crime, Iyemon accuses the man of stealing a family heirloom, using this as a pretext for murdering him. He then nails the bodies of Oiwa and the servant to two sides of a wooden door, which he throws into a nearby river. Now he can receive his new bride. In the play, as the wedding celebration begins, Iyemon approaches the girl and lifts her headdress, only to look into the horrific visage of Oiwa. The startled bridegroom draws his sword, slashing off the bride's head. He then runs to tell her grandfather, but blocking his path is his murdered servant. Iyemon strikes out again, only to find that he has cut off the head of his neighbor.

In another version, the ghost of Oiwa begins to haunt the new lovers night after night, wailing and howling in ghostly misery. Unable to stand the torment of this vengeful apparition any longer, the samurai one evening rushes out into the yard, sword in hand. There, standing before him, is the figure of his murdered wife, her twisted face visible in the moonlight. Crazed, the samurai advances and strikes her dead. At last, he has gotten rid of Oiwa, once and for all. Yet, as he rolls the body over in triumph, he screams with a terrible terror. At his feet lies the still-warm corpse of his new wife.

The kabuki play shows Iyemon being relentlessly

pursued by Oiwa. Her twisted face appears everywhere, even in a lantern which sways over his head. There is no escape from her ghost. One day he goes fishing in the river and hooks a large board. Predictably, it is the wooden door with the bodies of Oiwa and the servant nailed to it. Completely broken, Iyemon retreats to a mountain cottage. But even here there is no peace. Around him, vines and ropes come alive as writhing snakes. Flowers seem like accusing eyes. Smoke turns into strands of Oiwa's hair. Iyemon, by now, welcomes his own death, which finally comes at the hands of Oiwa's brother.

But while Iyemon's other victims might have been avenged, Oiwa's ghost seems unappeased. In modern Japan, for example, legend has it that there are many odd happenings whenever a movie is made about her life. As a ghost story *Yotsuya Kaidan* remains enormously popular, still performed today on stage and in film. Japanese people look forward to the special version which is aired at midnight each August during Obon. And so far, it is said, every movie production has encountered a series of inexplicable problems both on and off the set. For instance, there was the film that disappeared, the series of fires, and the several mysterious mechanical failures. These goings-on always stopped as soon as the cast, the film crew, and especially the actors and actresses visited Oiwa's shrine in Yotsuya to pay respects.

Despite several troubling occurrences on the set, one director reportedly dismissed it all as superstitious nonsense—until he fell and broke both his legs. And the actor Peter Alexander's imitation of Oiwa was said to be so effective that coactors and friends warned him about appeasing her spirit. The writer Denny Sargent recalls being invited to Alexander's home one evening to witness the havoc wreaked in the room, with several large

potted plants uprooted and a folding screen thrown over
and ripped in numerous places. Yet there were no signs
of forced entry or even the slightest wind to explain the
damage. A journey to Oiwa's shrine restored peace to this
actor's life, and there has been no similar trouble since.

But although she can be very scary for adults who
meet her on a dark, Tokyo street, Oiwa is believed able to
protect women and children. Her grave in Sugamo and

Countless pilgrims have visited the grave of
Oiwa, perhaps the most famous ghost in Tokyo.

her shrine in Yotsuya are constantly filled with devotional offerings of candles and flowers. There is also supposed to be an unknown woman who has spent her entire life taking care of Oiwa's grave. And so in Tokyo today the Oiwa mystery remains, a haunting reminder of a love gone wrong.

Another favorite tale is *Bancho Sarayashiki,* about a plate-counting ghost called Okiku. This story has many versions. Sometimes Okiku is a servant falsely accused of breaking a plate by a jealous wife. Or she is the daughter of the owner of the plates, and is thrown into a well for breaking one of them. Or she is the object of lust of a samurai who uses the number of plates as an excuse for murdering her and throwing her body down a well. The hapless Okiku returns as a ghost pathetically counting the plates, which should number ten: one plate, two plates, three plates, four plates, five plates, six plates, seven plates, eight plates, nine plates. The ghost then sobs frantically before she begins counting again, a pattern repeated over and over in her desperation to find the missing tenth plate. In one story a friend of the family who heard about the haunting waited at night until Okiku started counting. When she reached nine and before she could sob, he jumped out and shouted "TEN!" With this he frees the ghost from her obsession and puts her to rest.

A poignant rendering of the Okiku story is written by Kido Okamoto. Here Okiku is a servant in the house of Aoyama Harima, a samurai who boasts a precious heirloom in his set of ten Korean dishes. It was believed that if all ten dishes were broken, then the Aoyama family would meet total ruin.

Aoyama is in love with his servant, and has promised her marriage, but Okiku remains doubtful of his sincerity. She decides to test his love by deliberately breaking one dish and saying it was an accident. The Aoyama family also deemed that whoever broke one of the precious plates would be put to death, but Aoyama refused to kill Okiku. The family's old retainer, Judayu, however, learns that a servant had witnessed Okiku smashing the plate against a pillar and informs Aoyama, who questions her again. Okiku admits she did it to test his love for her. Aoyama is furious and prepares to kill her. When asked by two other servants to spare her life, Aoyama explains that it is not just a matter of broken plates. He orders them to bring several other plates, which he himself breaks. He then unsheathes his sword and kills Okiku. Thereafter the blue light of her *hito dama* is seen hovering above the well in the garden. The fortunes of the Aoyama family go from bad to worse until at last the day comes when Aoyama is forced to commit suicide. Before dying he takes a stroll in the garden where he encounters the *hito dama* and also the ghost of Okiku. Asking her to show her face he sees that it is beautiful and calm, bearing no grudge against him. Taking strength from this he calls for his two oldest servants, the faithful Judayu and Gonji, offering them money and the chance to find a new master. Gonji refuses and decides to commit seppuku, after Aoyama. Judayu opts to become a monk. And Aoyama kills himself and joins the spirit of Okiku in eternity.